Practical
Hotel English

김 종 견

백산출판사

CONTENTS

UNIT 1

Hotel Reservations

UNIT 1

Hotel Reservations

Dialogue 1

A: I'd like a room for two people, for three nights please.

B: Ok, I just need you to fill in this form please. Do you want breakfast?

A: Yes, please.

B: Breakfast is from 8 to 10 each morning in the dining room. Here is your key. Your room number is 2135, on the third floor. Enjoy your stay.

A: Thank you.

Dialogue 2

A: I'd like a room please.

B: Do you have a reservation?

A: No, I don't.

B: How many nights?

A: Two nights, please.

B: For two people?

A: Yes.

B: Do you want breakfast?

A: No, thank you.

B: Ok, that will be $430. Do you want to pay now, or when you check out?

A: I'll pay now.

B: Can you fill this in, and sign here please.
Thank you. Here is your receipt and your key. You are in room 3211, on the second floor.

Dialogue 3

A: Walker Hill Hotel. Can I help you?[1)]

B: Hello, I would like a room for Friday, March 10th.

A: What kind of room would you like?

B: I'd like a single room, please.

A: Hold on, please ······. I'm afraid all our single rooms are reserved.
The only room we have available is a twin.

B: How much for the twin room?

A: 350 dollars including tax.

B: Does that include breakfast?

A: No, but breakfast is available in our dining room.

B: OK, I'll take a room for tonight.

A: I'll need to get your credit card information to guarantee your room···.

---

1) Chain Hotels:
When choosing a hotel for a longer stay or a vacation abroad, many people look first to those with the most famous names. Whatever country you live in, the brand names Hilton, Radisson, Best Western, Marriott, or Ritz Carlton, for example, are likely to be familiar. Often starting with just one hotel, each of these companies have invested in other properties, to create a chain of hotels.
Although they may be located in many different countries, the main feature of these chain hotels is that each hotel (of the same name) can be expected to offer the same level of comfort and hospitality. For many guests, the hotel name alone is enough to convince them to make a booking.

Dialogue 4

A: Good afternoon, Hills Hotel. May I help you?[2)]

B: Yes. I'd like to book a room, please.

A: Certainly. When for, madam?

B: March the 23rd.

A: How long will you be staying?

B: Three nights.

A: What kind of room would you like, madam?

B: Double with bath. I'd appreciate it if you could give me a room with a view over the lake.

A: Certainly, madam. I'll just check what we have available. Yes, we have a room on the 5th floor with a really splendid view.

B: Fine. How much is the charge per night?

A: Would you like breakfast?

B: No, thanks.

A: It's 389 dollars per night excluding VAT.

B: That's fine.

---

2) Resort Hotels:

Of course, even a great name is not enough if a hotel is not in the right location!

Resort Hotels are so called because they cater to people who want to stay in popular holiday destinations. Traditionally, the seaside and the mountains are preferred locations. Coastal towns and mountain villages in many countries were known as 'resorts' long before the big hotels moved in, but sometimes it is the arrival of one of the larger, well known hotels that indicates the development of a new resort. The hotel itself then becomes the main center of activity, providing all the facilities, entertainment and home comforts a guest desires, with no need to venture outside the hotel grounds at all.

Typically, a resort hotel will contain a selection of different room types of varying prices. The cost of a room will depend on such things as its size and the number of beds it contains, as well as the time of year (the holiday season) and the number of consecutive nights booked. Many resort hotels offer package deals, where prices might also include all food and soft drinks taken over the course of a guest's stay.

The better and higher rated (four and five star) hotels generally offer rooms containing all the necessary amenities, such as television, mini-bar, safe, ironing board, hair dryer, bath robes and complimentary toiletries. Room service allows guests to take meals in their rooms, if they choose. Shared facilities are likely to include swimming pools, restaurants and bars. Luxury brand Resort and Spa hotels will also have fitness and spa treatment centers, offering a variety of (sometimes very exotic!) treatments, all either at an extra charge or included as part of a 'package'.

A: Who's the booking for, please, madam?

B: James

A: Okay, let me make sure I got that: James. Double with bath for March the 23rd, 24th and 25th. Is that correct?

B: Yes it is. Thank you.

A: Let me give you your confirmation number. It's: 897632. I'll repeat that: 897632. Thank you for choosing Hills Hotel and have a nice day. Goodbye.

B: Goodbye.

Dialogue 5

A: Thanks for calling Hills. James speaking.

B: Hello. I'm interested in booking a room for the October long weekend.

A: I'm afraid we're totally booked for that weekend. There's a convention in town and we're the closest hotel to the convention centre.

B: Oh, I didn't realize. Well what about the weekend after that?

A: So... Friday the fifteenth?

B: Yes. Friday and Saturday.

A: It looks like we have a few vacancies left. We recommend that you make a reservation, though. It's still considered peak season then.

B: Okay. Do you have any rooms with two double beds? We're a family of five.

A: Yes, all of our rooms have two double beds. The rate for that weekend is $455 dollars a night.

B: That's reasonable. And do you have cots? One of my daughters might be bringing a friend.

A: We do, but we also charge an extra 20 dollars per person for any family with over five people. The cot is free.

B: Okay, but I'm not positive if she is coming. Can we pay when we arrive?

A: Yes, but we do require a fifty dollar credit card deposit to hold the room. You can cancel up to five days in advance and we will refund your deposit.

B: Great, I'll call you right back. I have to find my husband's credit card.

A: Okay. Oh, and just to let you know... our outdoor pool will be closed, but our indoor pool is open.

Dialogue 6

A: Hills Hotel. May I help you?

B: Yes, please give me the reservation desk.

A: One moment, please.

C: Good afternoon, reservation desk. May I help you, sir?

B: This is James from LA. I'd like to reserve a room, please.

C: What are the dates of your visit, sir?

B: I'll be there tonight and check out Wednesday morning.

C: What type of room do you want, sir?

B: A double room with a river view.

C: Very good, sir. We have a nice room available.

B: What's the rate of a double room?

C: 349 dollars per night. The government tax and service charges will be added to this rate.

B: I'll take it. I'll be there by 6 o'clock.

C: Thank you for calling. We shall be waiting for you.

Dialogue 7

A: Good morning, Hills hotel. May I help you, sir?

B: I'd like to book a room, please.

A: When for, sir?

B: March 19th.

A: How long will you plan to stay?

B: Three nights.

A: What kind of room would you like, sir?

B: A double room on a higher floor with a nice view, please.

A: Can you give me your name, please?

B: James.

A: I'm sorry, I didn't get the name. Will you spell it for me, please?

B: J-A-M-E-S

A: Mr. James a double room on 10th floor for the 19th and 21st of March.

B: That's right. Thank you. Good bye.

A: Thank you for calling.

Dialogue 8

A: Good afternoon. Welcome to The Lotte Hotel.

B: Hi, Good afternoon. I'd like to make a reservation for the second weekend in November. Do you have any vacancies?

A: We have several rooms available for that particular weekend. And what is the exact date of your arrival?

B: The 15th.

A: How long will you be staying?

B: I'll be staying for three nights.

A: How many people is the reservation for?

B: There will be three of us.

A: Would you like a room with twin beds or a double bed?

B: Twin beds, please.

A: Would you prefer to have a room with a view of the river?

B: If that type of room is available, I would like to have a river view. What's the rate for the room?

A: Your room is 255 dollars per night. What name will the reservation be listed under?

B: James Choi.

A: Would you spell your last name for me, please?

B: Okay. C-H-O-I

A: Is there a phone number where you can be contacted?

B: My cell phone number is 010-3346-5898.

A: I'll need your credit card information to reserve the room for you.
What type of card is it?

B: Visa. The number is 8392 3402 3581 3890.

A: What is the name of the cardholder?

B: James Choi.

A: Okay, Mr. Choi, your reservation has been made for the 15th of November for a room with twin beds and view of the river. Check-in is at 2 o'clock. If you have any other questions, please do not hesitate to call us.

B: Thank you so much.

A: My pleasure. We'll see you in November, Mr. Choi. Have a good day.

Dialogue 9

A: Thanks for calling Lotte hotel. John speaking.

B: Hello. I'm interested in booking a room for the December long weekend.

A: I'm afraid we're totally booked for that weekend. There's a convention in town and we're the closest hotel to the convention centre.

B: Oh, I didn't realize. Well what about the weekend after that?

A: So... Saturday the 15th?

B: Yes. Saturday and Sunday.

A: It looks like we have a few vacancies left. We recommend that you make a reservation, though. It's still considered peak season then.

B: Okay. Do you have any rooms with two twin beds? We're a family of five.

A: Yes, all of our rooms have two twin beds. The rate for that weekend is $355 dollars a night.

B: That's reasonable. And do you have cots? One of my sons might be bringing a friend.

A: We do, but we also charge an extra 20 dollars per person for any family with over five people. The cot is free.

B: Okay, but I'm not positive if he is coming. Can we pay when we arrive?

A: Yes, but we do require 30 dollars credit card deposit to hold the room. You can cancel up to three days in advance and we will refund your deposit.

B: Great, I'll call you right back.

A: Okay. Oh, and just to let you know... our outdoor pool will be closed, but our indoor pool is open.

Dialogue 10

A: Lotte Hotel. Can I help you?[3)]

B: Yes. I am interested in getting some information about accommodation for some friends coming from USA.

A: What kind of information would you like?

B: Well. I was wondering whether it would be cheaper for a family of four to get two double rooms and one single room or to get a suite?

A: I would think that the suite might be more economical and more comfortable for the four of them.

---

3) Business and Conference Hotels:

Business and Conference Hotels (as you might have guessed!) are those that have been designed with business clients in mind. They are often located in designated business areas of large cities, with easy access to exhibition centers and city transport links. The main function of business and conference hotels is the provision of all the services and facilities related to the carrying on of 'business as usual', whilst key corporate executives Business and Conference Hotels:

Business and Conference Hotels (as you might have guessed!) are those that have been designed with business clients in mind. They are often located in designated business areas of large cities, with easy access to exhibition centers and city transport links. The main function of business and conference hotels is the provision of all the services and facilities related to the carrying on of 'business as usual', whilst key corporate executives and their staff are away from their regular workplace.

The growth of global business has led to an increasing demand from corporate clients for accommodation tailored specifically to the needs of busy executives and management teams. Large corporations often choose to hold their annual general meetings, or stage training sessions or exhibitions in locations that are convenient and accessible to large numbers of national and international company employees. Business and Conference hotels are expected to satisfy both the work and the leisure needs of their guests for the duration of such events.

Rooms in this type of hotel are designed with businessmen and women in mind and always provide, along with all the expected comforts, work areas with office supplies and wi-fi connections. Common areas in these hotels are likely to include large meeting rooms, with all the latest audio-visual technology installed, staffed office spaces for the sending and receiving of faxes, or for photocopying and distribution of documents, as well as access to external courier services, such as FedEx, UPS or DHL.

Other facilities and services include: banquet halls for large formal dinners, provision of snacks during breaks in meetings, and the availability of fully equipped fitness centers – in which business guests may burn off excess calories from the previous day's 'Informal Business Lunch'.

Business and conference hotels depend, more than any other hotel type, on establishing ongoing relationships with their clients and are often fully booked, well ahead of important local exhibitions and Trade Fairs. Such events can fill even the largest of cities to bursting point, and make the finding of even a single hotel room a virtual impossibility.

B: Have you got a three - room suite?

A: I'm sorry. We haven't got any three-room suite but we have got a penthouse which is very luxurious. And a two- room suite…

B: How much would two - room suite cost?

A: For one night, the cost would be 350 dollars included breakfast.

B: By the way, have you got a play ground for children in your hotel compound?

A: There's no problem about that. Our hotel is very modern and we're fully equipped with recreational facilities.

B: I will talk to my friend and let you know?

A: Fine, madam. We hope to hear from you soon.

B: Thank you. Goodbye.

A: Good bye.

Dialogue 11

A: Hills hotel. May I help you?

B: I want to book a double room. We'll be in Seoul on February 19th, but I'm not sure how long we'll stay.

A: Alright. But we can only confirm a room for you from the 19th to the 23th. After that we'll be fully booked.

B: Fully booked? Why's that?

A: The Seoul Festival will be getting under way.

B: What if we want to stay past the 23th?

A: I'm afraid we'll be full. But we can always try to find another hotel for you.

B: Thank you. And could you tell me how much you charge per night?

A: 355 dollars for a double.

B: Does the room come with a complimentary breakfast?

A: Yes, a free buffet breakfast is included in the room rate.

B: Alright. I want to make a reservation.

A: May I ask who the booking is for, please?

B: Mr. and Mrs. James.

A: And how can we contact you?

B: You can reach me at 010-3309-5892.

A: Very good, sir. We're looking forward to your visit on February 17th, Mr. James.

Useful Expressions

- Do the rooms have refrigerators?
- Do you do group bookings?
- Is there an outdoor pool?
- Do you have any cheaper rooms?
- When is it considered off- season?
- Do you charge extra for two beds?
- How much is it for a cot?
- Do you offer free breakfast?
- Is there a restaurant in the hotel?
- I'd like to make a reservation for next week.
- Is it necessary to book ahead?
- We serve a continental breakfast.
- Cable television is included, but the movie channel is extra.
- Take Exit 7 off the highway and you'll see us a few kilometers up on the left hand side.
- The rate I can give you is 159 dollars with tax.
- We require a credit card number for a deposit.
- We advise that you book in advance during peak season.
- Will two double beds be enough?
- Do you want a smoking or non-smoking room?
- The dining room is open from 5 pm until 9 pm.
- We have an indoor swimming pool and sauna.
- How many adults will be in the room?
- I'm afraid we are booked that weekend.
- There are only a few vacancies left.
- Lotte Hotel, James speaking. How can I help you?
- What date are you looking for?
- How long will you be staying?

- Lotte Hotels, James speaking. How can I help you?
- What date are you looking for?
- How long will you be staying?
- How many adults will be in the room?
- I'm afraid we are booked that weekend.
- There are only a few vacancies left.
- We advise that you book in advance during peak season.
- Will two double beds be enough?
- Do you want a smoking or non-smoking room?
- The dining room is open from 5 pm until 10 pm.
- We have an indoor swimming pool and sauna.
- We serve a continental breakfast.
- Cable television is included, but the movie channel is extra.
- Take Exit 7 off the highway and you'll see us a few kilometers up on the left hand side.
- The rate I can give you is 345 with tax.
- We require a credit card number for a deposit.
- I'd like to make a reservation for next week.
- Is it necessary to book ahead?
- Do you charge extra for two beds?
- How much is it for a cot?
- Do you offer free breakfast?
- Is there a restaurant in the hotel?
- Do the rooms have refrigerators?
- Do you do group bookings?
- Is there an outdoor pool?
- Do you have any cheaper rooms?
- When is it considered off- season?

2
UNIT

Hotel Front Desk

2
UNIT

Hotel Front Desk

Dialogue 1

A: Good afternoon. How can I help you?

B: Good afternoon. Actually I am looking for a room in your hotel. So can you provide me information regarding that?

A: Sure sir. We have a room which will cost you 456 dollars per day. In which you will get breakfast buffet complimentary.

B: Is the price negotiable?

A: If you will pay by debit or credit card so you will get 15% cash back.

B: Will I get discount on online booking?

A: Yes sir you will get 20% discount on that.

B: So how much will it cost?

A: It will cost you around 399 dollars plus taxes per day

B: OK.

A: How long are you planning your stay?

B: For three nights.

A: So when will you check-in?

B: Tomorrow.

A: Sir, you have to pay one day advance at the time of check-in.

B: Why so?

A: Sir, this is the policy of our hotel and we have to adhere to it

B: OK, no problem.

A: Sure Sir.

B: Thank you.

Dialogue 2

A: Front desk. May I help you?

B: Hi, I'm in 3114 and my TV doesn't seem to be working.

A: We will send someone up to take a look at it in a few minutes. How is everything else?

B: Everything else with the room is great. Do the rooms come equipped with irons?

A: No, but they are available free of charge here at the front desk.

B: What should I do with iron when I'm finished?

A: You can keep it in your room. If you don't here back from me before 10 tonight, just leave it on your desk and the cleaning staff will pick it up in the morning.

B: OK, thanks for everything.

A: Enjoy your stay, and don't hesitate to call if there is something else I can do for you.

Dialogue 3

A: Hi! So that's James. How would you like to pay for the room?

B: Do you take VISA?

A: Yes, we do. We take VISA, Mastercard, and American Express.

B: I'll pay with VISA then. What time is checkout?

A: Checkout is at 12 o'clock. Your room number is 3114. Is there anything else you would like to know?

B: What time do the restaurants close?
A: 9 p.m. There are restaurants on the 2nd and 3rd floor and there's a cafe next to the lobby.
B: Is there a pool here?
A: No, we don't.

Dialogue 4

A: Operator. May I help you?
B: Yes. How do I get an outside line, please?
A: Just dial 0, wait for the dial tone, and then dial the phone number you want to call. Or we can place a call for you, if you want.
B: No, thanks a lot. I'll try it myself.

Dialogue 5

A: Front Desk. James speaking. How may I help you, Mr. John?
B: Hello. Is it possible to change my room?
I want to move closer to my parents' room. They are staying in room 1342.
Do you have something like an adjoining room next to them?
A: Let me check.
We have a room on the 5th floor. It is on the opposite side of the hall.
Is that okay with you?
B: Okay. That's good. I will take it.
A: All right, sir.
When would you like to change your room?
B: Anytime is fine.
A: I will send a bellman up to your room and have him move your stuff to the new room.
B: Thank you.
A: You're welcome, sir.

Dialogue 6

A: Good afternoon, sir. Can I help you with anything?
B: I don't have a reservation. Do you have a room available for three nights?
A: I will check for you.
We have a twin room available for three nights.
B: Okay, thanks. I will take it.
A: All right. May I have your picture ID and a credit card to secure the reservation, please?
B: Okay.

Dialogue 7

A: Hello, thank you for calling the Lotte Hotel. My name is James.[4]
How can I help you?
B: Hi. I made a reservation with you a couple of weeks ago and I need to change it to a different date. Can I do that?
A: Let me bring you up on the system here. Do you have a reservation number?
B: A reservation number?

---

4) •Have you got a single room for tonight?
•I'd like to stay in a double room.
•Do all the rooms have air-conditioning?
•Is breakfast included?
•When do you serve breakfast?
•Could you give me a call at 7 tomorrow morning, please?
•I'd like to pay in cash/by credit card/by traveller's cheque.
• Hello, can I help you?
•Would you like a room with a bath or a shower?
•How long would you like to stay at our hotel?
•How would you like to pay?
•Your room is on the second floor on the right.
•Sorry, we're fully booked for tonight.
•Sorry, we are full up.
•Is there anything else I can do for you?

A: You would have received that when you called the first time.

B: No, I don't. Uh, I don't think I ever got one.

A: Oh, that's no problem. I can look you up on the system. Uh, what's the last name on the reservation?

B: The last name is James. That's J-a-m-e-s.

A: And what's your arrival date?

B: November 5th.

A: Ok, here you are. And so you'd like to cancel this reservation?

B: I just need to change the date.

A: Yeah, we can do that. Uh, to when would you like to change it?

B: Do you have anything for December 10th?

A: December 10th? OK, let me check. Unfortunately, it seems that all of our rooms are booked for that entire week.

B: You don't have anything available at all?

A: We do, but not in a non-smoking Standard Room. Uh, we have a non-smoking Deluxe Executive.

B: So how much is the uh, the Deluxe Executive again?

A: It's $850 plus tax.

B: Now I remember why I didn't take it last time.

A: Well, would you like to take the Standard Room that's available?

B: But you said that room was smoking, right?

A: Yes, sir.

B: I can't stand the smell of smoke so I'm going to have to pass on that.

A: I understand, sir.

B: Well, are those the only two rooms you've got? You don't have anything else?

A: No, I'm sorry. That's a very busy time for us because we host a lot of conventions at that time of year.

B: Alright, well, I guess if I can't get a room at that time then I'll have to cancel after all.

A: No problem, sir. I just need the credit card number that you used to make the reservation with.

B: Yeah, sure, it's uh, it's 8392 3921 3871 4231.

A: OK, that does it. I've cancelled your reservation now. Uh, I'm sorry we couldn't accommodate the change for you this time.

B: No, that's ok. Thanks.

A: Thank you for choosing our hotel. Please call again the next time you visit.

B: I will.

A: Have a good day, sir.

B: Thanks. You too.

A: Good bye.

B: See you next time.

3
UNIT

Hotel Checking-In

3
UNIT

Hotel Checking-In

Dialogue 1

A: Good morning. Welcome to Hills Hotel. Can I help you?

B: I have a reservation for today. It's under the name of James.

A: Can you please spell that for me, sir?

B: Sure. J-A-M-E-S.

A: Yes, Mr. James, we've reserved a double room for you with a view of the ocean for three nights. Is that correct?

B: Yes, it is.

A: OK. We already have your credit card information on file. If you'll just sign the receipt along the bottom, please.

B: 443 dollars a night!

A: Yes, sir. We are a five star hotel after all.

B: OK. I'm here on business anyway, so at least I'm staying on the company's dime. What's included in this cost anyway?

A: A full american breakfast every morning, airport shuttle service, and use of the hotel's safe are all included.

B: So what's not included in the price?

A: Well, you will find a mini-bar in your room. Use of it will be charged to your account. Also, the hotel provides room service, at an additional charge of course.

B: So what room am I in?

A: Room 2341. Here is your key. To get to your room, take the elevator on the left up to the 10th floor. Turn right once you exit the elevator and your room will be on the right hand side. A bellboy will bring your bags up shortly.

B: Thank you.

A: Would you have any questions or requests, please dial 'O' from your room. Also, there is internet available in the lobby 24 hours a day.

B: What time is check-out?

A: At 12 o'clock, sir.

B: Thank you.

A: My pleasure, sir. Have a wonderful stay at Hills Hotel.

Dialogue 2

A: Good afternoon, welcome to Hills hotel.

B: Hi.

A: How can I help you today?

B: I need to check in.

A: Of course sir, My name is James and I'll be your guest representative during your stay. Could I have your name please?

B: Johnson.

A: Yes Mr. Johnson, here you are. And how are you today?

B: Tired actually, it was a very long flight.

A: Well, I'll get you checked in as soon as possible so you can relax.[5]

---

5) More Formal expressions
Goodbye
Thank you for coming. Have a pleasant day.
Goodbye, please come again.
Goodbye, I hope to see you again.

Dialogue 3

A: Hello. Mr. James. One moment, please. Yes, here it is.
One single room for three nights.
B: That's right. Could I have a room on a lower floor, please?
I don't like to use the lift.
A: Are you OK with the third floor?[6)]
B: Yes, that's wonderful. Thank you.
A: Could I have your credit card, please?
B: Yes, here's my VISA card.
A: Thanks. This will just take a minute. Here's your credit card. You're in Room 3303. Please sign here. And would you like a wake-up call?
B: Oh, yes. Could I have a wake-up call at 6:00 tomorrow, please?
A: Of course. Would you like a newspaper?
B: Yes, I'd like Seoul Times every morning, please. And what time's breakfast?
A: Breakfast is between 6-10.
B: Thanks.
A: Enjoy your stay, Mr. James.

Dialogue 4

A: Hi, my name is James and I have a reservation for tonight.
B: Let me check. OK, yes. A twin room for two nights.
A: That's right.

Less Formal Goodbyes
See you later (soon) So long
Good bye (bye) Please come again
I have to run I have to be going now
Catch you later See you again

6) British English American English the 10th floor = the 11th floor the 9th floor = the 10th floor the 8th floor = the 9th floor the 7th floor = the 8th floor the 6th floor = the 7th floor the 5th floor = the 6th floor the 4th floor = the 5th floor the 3rd floor = the 4th floor the 2nd floor = the 3rd floor the 1st floor = the 2nd floor the ground floor = the 1st floor the basement = the basement

B: You are in room 3114. How would you like to pay for the room?

A: Do you take American Express Travelers Checks?

B: Certainly, are they in American funds?

A: No, in Canadian. Is that OK?

B: Yes, no problem. With the exchange, that comes to 345 dollars Canadian.

A: Do I pay now or when I check out.

B: In advance, please.

A: Here you go.

B: The elevator is just around the corner. Do you need any help with your bags?

A: No thanks. I can manage myself.

B: Is there anything else we can do to help you enjoy your stay?

A: Can you give me a wake-up call at 6:00?

B: We don't do that from here.

A: Oh, yes. I have a meeting downtown tomorrow. Does this hotel have a shuttle bus?

B: No, I'm afraid we don't, but we will be happy to call a taxi for you if you provide us with the details.

A: No, that won't be necessary. I can call from my room.

B: There are no charges for local calls.

Dialogue 5[7)]

A: Good afternoon. Welcome to the Lotte Hotel. How may I help you?

B: I have a reservation for today. It's under the name of James Choi.

---

7) • More Formal expressions

Goodbye

Thank you for coming. Have a pleasant day.

Goodbye, please come again.

Goodbye, I hope to see you again.

• Less Formal Goodbyes

See you later (soon)	So long
Good bye	Bye
I have to run	I have to be going now
Catch you later	Later
See you again	Please come again

A: Can you please spell that for me, sir?

B: Sure. C-H-O-I.

A: Yes, Mr. Choi, we've reserved a twin room for you with a view of the river for three nights. Is that correct?

B: Yes, it is.

A: We already have your credit card information on file. If you'll just sign the receipt along the bottom, please.

B: 355 dollars a night!

A: Yes, sir. We are a five star hotel after all.

B: Well, fine. I'm here on business anyway, so at least I'm staying on the company's dime. What's included in this cost anyway?

A: A full Continental buffet every morning, free airport shuttle service, and use of the hotel's safe are all included.

B: So what's not included in the price?

A: Well, you will find a mini-bar in your room. Use of it will be charged to your account. Also, the hotel provides room service, at an additional charge of course.

B: Hmm. Ok, so what room am I in?

A: Room 1523. Here is your key. To get to your room, take the elevator on the right up to the fifth floor. Turn left once you exit the elevator and your room will be on the left hand side. A bellboy will bring your bags up shortly.

B: Great. Thank you.

A: Should you have any questions or requests, please dial 'O' from your room. Also, there is internet available in the lobby 24 hours a day.

B: Ok, and what time is check-out?

A: At midday, sir.

B: Ok, thanks.

A: My pleasure, sir. Have a wonderful stay at the Lotte Hotel.

Dialogue 6

A: Good afternoon, Sir. Can I help you?

B: Good afternoon. Can I get a room in the Hotel please?

A: Have you made an advance booking, Sir?

B: I'm afraid I haven't done any room reservation. I tried to do hotel online booking. I believe that hotel reservation software was not working then

A: What kind of a room do you want, Sir? A double room or a single room?

B: A single room, please.

A: Let me see. (Looking at the register). We are fully booked up at this time of the year. No, we haven't a single room available, sir.

B: But please do try to help me out. I wouldn't know where else to stay.

Dialogue 7

A: Good morning, welcome to Lotte Hotel, how may I help you?

B: Good morning, I would like to stay here.

A: Do you have any reservation before, Sir?

B: No, I don't have.

A: May I know what type of room do you want to get, for how long time and how many person Sir?

B: I want to reserve one standard twin bed room for three nights, it's from 5th January until 8th January and that's for one person.

A: Wait a moment please Sir, I would like to check the room available that you want on that period.

B: Yes, please ···

*** Few second later ***

A: Thank you for your waiting Sir, you're very lucky because, one standard twin bed room still available on that period. May I explain to you about room and hotel facilities, Sir?

B: Yes, please ···

A: The room facilities in our hotel such as private balcony, living room, kitchenette, refrigerator with mini bar, wardrobe, television, Telephone with telephone

attention, air conditioner and safety deposit box.
The room rate is 659 dollars include breakfast.

Well Sir, would you like to take this room?

B: Yes, I take this room.
A: Well Sir, please fill this registration card, this is your pen and this is your welcome drink, please enjoy it!
B: Ok, Thank you.

(Reception fills the guest card and breakfast coupon)

B: I've finished filling the registration card.
A: Thank you, may I check your registration card, please?
B: Yes, of course.
A: Well, your name is Mr. James and your room number is 1457, the room rate is 600 dollars included breakfast and your departure date is 8th January, is that right, Sir?
B: Yes, that's right
A: This is your room key and guest card. First of all, if you would like going to outside hotel, please keep your room key in the receptionist desk.
This is you breakfast coupon. If you would like to have a breakfast, please come to restaurant. It's open from 06:30 A.M until 09:30 A.M, and don't forget to bring your breakfast coupon at the cashier.
B: Yes, thank you for your information.

Useful Expressions

- What time's the restaurant open for dinner?
- Dinner's served between 6pm and 9.30pm
- What time does the bar close?
- Would you like any help with your luggage?

- Would you like a newspaper?
- Would you like a wake-up call?
- What time's breakfast?
- Breakfast's from 7am till 10am
- Could I have breakfast in my room, please?
- I've got a reservation
- Could I see your passport?
- Could you please fill in this registration form?
- My booking was for a double room

Hotel Words

word *part of speech*	meaning and example sentences
adjoining rooms *noun*	two hotel rooms with a door in the centre If you want we can book your parents in an adjoining room.
amenities *noun*	local facilities such as stores and restaurants We are located downtown, so we are close to all of the amenities.
attractions *noun*	things for tourists to see and do The zoo is our city's most popular attraction for kids.
baggage *noun*	bags and suitcases packed with personal belongings If you need help with your baggage we have a cart you can use.
Bed and Breakfast *noun*	a home that offers a place to stay and a place to eat I can book you into a beautiful Bed and Breakfast on the lake.
bellboy *noun*	a staff member who helps guests with their luggage The bellboy will take your bags to your room for you.
book *verb*	arrange to stay in a hotel I can book your family in for the weekend of the seventh.
booked *adj*	full, no vacancies I'm afraid the hotel is booked tonight.
brochures *noun*	small booklets that provide information on the local sites and attractions Feel free to take some brochures to your room to look at.
check-in *verb*	go to the front desk to receive keys You can check-in anytime after four o'clock.
check-out *noun*	return the keys and pay for the bill Please return your parking pass when you check-out.
complimentary breakfast *noun*	free of charge All of our rooms have complimentary soap, shampoo, and coffee.
cot, rollaway bed *noun*	a single bed on wheels that folds up If you need an extra bed, we have cots available.
floor *noun*	a level of the building The swimming pool is on the main floor.
front desk, reception *noun*	the place where guests go to check in and out and to get information Towels are available at the front desk.
guest *noun*	a person that is staying at the hotel Our washrooms are for guests only.
damage charge *noun*	money a guest owes for repairs to hotel property (when caused by violent or careless acts) We will have to add a damage charge for the hole you put in the wall.
deposit *noun*	amount paid ahead of time to secure a reservation You will not receive your deposit back if you cancel.
double bed *noun*	a bed large enough for two people They are a family of four, so give them a room with two double beds.

hostel *noun*	a very inexpensive place for backpackers and travelers on a budget In the hostel you probably won't get your own room.
hotel manager *noun*	person in charge at the hotel I'll let you make your complaint to the hotel manager.
housekeeping maid*noun*	staff members that clean the rooms and linen Put a sign on the door if you want housekeeping to come in and change the sheets on the bed.
ice machine *noun*	a machine that automatically makes ice that guests can use to keep drinks cold There is an ice machine by the elevator on all of the even numbered floors.
indoor pool *noun*	place for guests to swim inside the hotel The heated indoor pool is open until 10 pm.
inn *noun*	another word for "hotel" There's an inn on the other side of town that has a vacancy.
Jacuzzi, hot tub, whirl pool *noun*	a small hot pool for relaxation Our honeymoon room has a personal hot tub.
king-size bed *noun*	extra large bed A room with a king size bed costs an extra ten dollars a night.
kitchenette *noun*	a small fridge and cooking area Your room has a kitchenette so you can prepare your own breakfasts and lunches.
late charge *noun*	a fee for staying past the check-out time You will be charged a ten dollar late charge for checking out after 11 am.
linen *noun*	sheets, blankets, pillow cases We will come in and change the linens while you are out of your room.
lobby *noun*	large open area at the front of the hotel You can stand in the lobby and wait for your bus.
luggage cart *noun*	a device on wheels that guests can push their luggage on Please return the luggage cart to the lobby when you are finished with it.
maximum capacity *noun*	the most amount of people allowed The maximum capacity in the hot tub is ten people.
motels *noun*	accommodations that are slightly cheaper than hotels Our motel is very clean and is close to the beach.
noisy *adj*	loud The guests next to you have complained that you are being too noisy.
parking pass *noun*	a piece of paper that guests display in the car window while in the hotel parking lot Display this parking pass in your window to show that you are a hotel guest.
pay-per-view movie *noun*	extra charge for movies and special television features If you order a pay-per-view movie, the charge will appear on your bill.

pillow case *noun*	the covering that goes over a pillow Room 201 doesn't need their sheets changed, but they requested one new pillow case.
queen size bed *noun*	bed with plenty of space for two people (bigger than a double) They have a queen size bed so the small child can easily fit in the middle.
rate *noun*	cost of renting a room for a certain time period Our rates change depending on the season.
reservation *noun*	a request to save a specific room for a future date They say they made a reservation but it doesn't show on the computer.
room service *noun*	delivery of food or other services requested by guests If you would like a bottle of wine, just call room service.
sauna *noun*	a hot room for relaxation, filled with steam We don't recommend bringing young children into the sauna.
single bed *noun*	a bed for one person The economy priced room includes one single bed.
sofa bed, pull-out couch *noun*	a bed built into a sofa or couch The room contains a sofa bed so the room actually sleeps five.
towels *noun*	used to cover and dry the body after swimming or bathing You can get your swimming pool towels at the front desk.
vacancy *noun* vacant *adj*	available rooms We only have one vacancy left, and it is for a single room.
valet *noun*	staff that parks the guests' vehicles If you leave your car keys with us, the valet will park your car underground.
vending machine *noun*	a machine that distributes snacks and beverages when you insert coins The vending machine on the fifth floor has chocolate bars and chips.
view *noun*	a window that offers a nice image for guests The room is more expensive because it has a spectacular view of the beach.
wake up call *noun*	a morning phone call from the front desk, acts as an alarm clock What time would you like your wake up call?
weight room, workout room, gym *noun*	a room that guests can use for exercise and fitness Our weight room has a stair climber and a stationary bicycle.

4

UNIT

Arriving at the Hotel

4

UNIT

Arriving at the Hotel[8]

Conversation 1

A: I'd like a room for three people, for two nights please.

B: Ok, I just need you to fill in this form please.

B: Do you want breakfast?

A: Yes, please.

8) Boutique Hotels:

The term 'Boutique Hotel' was first used by the owner of a famous hotel called Morgans, in the Manhattan district of New York. The concept behind the hotel was that it should appeal to guests searching for perfection in every detail of their hotel 'lifestyle experience' and that this experience should be very different from that offered by a traditional chain hotel.

Needless to say, the uniqueness of this first Boutique hotel, combined with the business ambition of its owners, resulted in the creation of a chain of Boutique hotels (Morgans Hotel Group) so that now some, once 'unique', features have become signature features, shared by each of the hotels within the group.

The original hotel's interior (as with all hotels in the group) was created by a world famous Interior Designer, and it is really this concentration on chic, artistic and luxurious accommodation, fixtures and fittings, that defines the character of this type of hotel. Boutique hotels attract guests who like to feel they are experiencing something that other more 'normal' hotel guests are either unlikely to appreciate, or perhaps unable to afford!

B: Breakfast is from 6 to 9 each morning in the dining room. Here is your key. Your room number is 1245, on the fifth floor. Enjoy your stay.

A: Thank you.

Conversation 2

A: I'd like a room please.

B: Do you have a reservation?

A: No, I don't.

B: How many nights?

A: Three nights, please.

B: For three people?

A: Yes.

B: Do you want breakfast?

A: No, thank you.

B: Ok, that will be $325. Do you want to pay now, or when you check out?

A: I'll pay now.

B: Can you fill this in, and sign here please.

B: Thank you. Here is your receipt and your key. You are in room 1434, on the fifth floor.

Conversation 3

A: I'd like to check out please.

B: What room number?

A: 1451.

B: That's $315 please.

James pays the hotel receptionist.

B: Thank you. Sign here please. Have a good journey.

A: Thank you.

Useful Expressions

- What time is breakfast?
- What time is check out?
- I'd like to check out, please.
- Can I see the room, please?
- Do you have a room with a bath?
- I'd like a room for three nights, please?
- Sorry, we're full. = Sorry, I don't have any rooms available.
- Your room number is 1235.
- Do you want a single room or a double room?
- Do you want breakfast?
- Do you have a reservation?
- How many nights?
- I'd like a room for 2 nights, please?
- Can I see the room, please?
- Do you have a room with a bath?
- What time is breakfast?
- What time is check out?
- I'd like to check out, please.
- Do you have a reservation?
- How many nights?
- Do you want a single room or a double room?
- Do you want breakfast?
- Sorry, we're full. = Sorry, I don't have any rooms available.
- Your room number is 3114.

UNIT 5

Hotel Check-out

5
UNIT

Hotel Check-out

Dialogue 1

A: Good morning. May I help you?[9]

B: Yes, I'd like to check out now. My name's James, room 2554. Here's the key.

A: One moment, please, sir. ... Here's your bill. Would you like to check and see if the amount is correct?

B: What's the 10 dollars for?

---

9) • IF GOOD
How are you? Great.
How's it going? Couldn't be better.
How has your day been? Fantastic.
• IF SO-SO
How have you been? Could be worse.
How's the family? Fair to middling.
Did you have a good day? I can't complain.
• IF BAD
How do you feel? Not too good.
How was your day? I've had better days.
Have you had a good day? No, it was lousy.

A: That's for the phone calls you made from your room.
B: Can I pay with traveller's cheques?
A: Certainly. May I have your passport, please?
B: Here you are.
A: Could you sign each cheque here for me?
B: Sure.
A: Here are your receipt and your change, sir. Thank you.
B: Thank you. Goodbye.

Dialogue 2

A: Hi there. Are you checking out now?
B: Yes, sorry. I know we're a few minutes late.
A: That's no problem. It's always really busy at check out time anyway.
B: Oh, really. The last hotel we stayed in charged us for a late check out.
A: The hotel isn't booked this week, so it's not a problem. How was everything?
B: The room was great. The beds were really comfortable, and we weren't expecting our own fridge.
A: I'm glad you liked it.
B: The kids were disappointed that the pool wasn't open this morning, though.
A: I apologize for that. We can't get a cleaner in any earlier than 11 am.
B: Well we had a nice swim last night anyhow.
A: Will you be putting this on your credit card?
B: No. I'll pay cash.
A: OK. So the total comes to $453,99 including tax.
B: I thought it was $400 even. That's what they said yesterday when we checked in.
A: Yes, but there is an extra room charge on your bill.
B: Oh, I forgot. My husband ordered a plate of nachos. Sorry.
A: No problem. So... from $140, here's your change. Now, I'll just need to ask you for your room keys.

Dialogue 3

A: I'd like to check out please.

B: What room number?

A: 3114.

B: That's $489 please.

James pays the hotel receptionist.

B: Thank you. Sign here please. Have a good journey.

A: Thank you.

Dialogue 4

A: Did you enjoy your stay with us?

B: Yes, very much so. However, I need to get to the airport. I have a flight that leaves in about three hours, so what is the quickest way to get there?

A: We do have a free airport shuttle service.

B: That sounds great, but will it get me to the airport on time?

A: Yes, it should. The next shuttle leaves in 30 minutes, and it takes approximately 45 minutes to get to the airport.

B: Fantastic. I'll just wait in the lounge area. Will you please let me know when it will be leaving?

A: Of course, sir. Before you go, would you be able to settle the mini-bar bill?

B: Oh yes certainly. How much will that be?

A: Let's see. The bill comes to $85. How would you like to pay for that?

B: I'll pay with my Visa thanks, but I'll need a receipt so I can charge it to my company.

A: Absolutely. Here we are sir. If you like you can leave your bags with the porter and he can load them onto the shuttle for you when it arrives.

B: That would be great thank you.

A: Would you like to sign the hotel guestbook too while you wait?

B: Sure, I had a really good stay here and I'll tell other people to come here.

A: That's good to hear. Thank you again for staying at The Lotte Hotel.

Useful Expressions

- What do you look for when choosing a hotel?
- Which features are the most important for you - swimming pool, sauna, good view, good food, internet connection, gym?
- Have you ever used room service?
- Have you ever had to lodge a complaint at a hotel?
- Have you ever had anything stolen at a hotel?
- Have you ever been upgraded to a better room?
- Are there any historic or luxurious ones?
- Do you prefer to stay in hotels in the city, countryside or seaside?
- What's the best hotel you've ever stayed in?
- What's the worst hotel you've stayed in?
- Have you ever been to a hotel with unique features?
- Have you ever stayed in a luxury hotel? What was it like?
- Have you ever been to a hotel for a special occasion, such as a wedding or conference?
- Have you ever worked at a hotel?
- Are there many hotels in your country?
  Do you like staying at hotels?
- How often do you stay at hotels?
- Do you normally stay at hotels for work/for pleasure?
- What's the longest you've ever stayed at the same hotel?
- double room
- twin room
- single room
- bar
- restaurant
- pool
- reception desk
- bed
- pillow
- blankets
- television

- door
- lights
- telephone
- ensuite bathroom
- towels
- tea and coffee making facilities
- key
- bar fridge
- safe
- air conditioner
- What name is the reservation under?
- How long will you be staying?
- Are you planning on checking out tomorrow?
- I'm afraid you can't check in until after 3:00 pm.
- What type of vehicle are you driving?
- Do you know the license plate number of your vehicle?
- Complimentary breakfast is served in the lobby between 7 and 9 am.
- I'll give you two room keys.
- The dining room is on the main floor at the end of the hall.
- The weight room and sauna are on the top floor.
- Just call the front desk if you need any extra towels or pillows.
- We have a reservation under James.
- Do you have any vacancies?
- Is the hotel booked, or can we get a room for tonight?
- How do we get to our room from here?
- Is it okay to park out front?
- What time is the pool open until?
- What time is breakfast served at?
- Is it too early to check in?
- Can we get a wake-up call?
- When is check out time?
- Are you ready to check out?
- What room were you in?
- How was your stay?

- Was everything satisfactory?
- Will you be putting this on your card?
- And how will you be paying for this?
- Would you like to speak to the hotel manager on duty?
- I'll just need your room keys, please.
- Enjoy the rest of your holiday.
- Have a safe trip home.
- We're checking out of room 2341.
- Sorry we're a bit late checking out.
- I'm afraid we overslept/slept in.
- We really enjoyed our stay.
- We have a few complaints.
- We'll be back next time we're in town.

6
UNIT

Hotel Housekeeping staff

6

UNIT

Hotel Housekeeping staff[10]

Dialogue 1

A: Excuse me, I just checked into my room, and there's hair in the tub and it's not mine. It's really gross.

B: Oh, I'm so sorry. That's not acceptable at all. I'll clean the tub for you immediately, or if you'd like, I can see if another room is available.

A: Thanks. If you clean it, that will be just fine. I have to go out. I'll be back in about 30 minutes.

(Phone rings)

C: Guest Services. This is James.

10) Doorman, Bellhop/Bellboy/Bellman, Concierge, Front Desk Clerk/Receptionist
Front Desk Manager, Cashier, Guest Relations Officer, Lift attendant
Cashier, Sales Manager, Housekeeper/Chambermaid/Maid
Laundry Staff, Room Service Staff, Maintenance Worker, Host/Hostess
Waiter/Waitress, Food and Beverage Manager, Executive Chef,
Fitness Center Attendant, Business Center Attendant, Event Planner, Operator
Reservation Agent, Driver, Valet

B: Hi, James; this is Jane. I just wanted to let you know that the guest in room 3421, Mrs. Susan, checked in today and found hair in her tub. But don't worry. I cleaned the tub, and it's spotless.

C: Thank you. I'll make sure and follow up with Mrs. Susan.

B: OK. Thanks.

Dialogue 2

A: Good afternoon, Hills, this is James. How may I help you?

B: Your people are so incredibly rude! All I wanted was a little extra sleep this morning because my son played tennis last night. But at 9 AM there was all this vacuuming outside my room. I went outside to ask the housekeeper to stop vacuuming. The woman — I don't know what her name was — said, "Sorry, lady, but I have to vacuum this area now. Relax, I'll be done soon." I couldn't believe it. I asked her again if she could vacuum later, but she said, "No, it has to be done now."

A: I am terribly sorry! You must be so tired, especially after playing tennis. I apologize that the attendant didn't understand that vacuuming would be so disturbing. I will call up there now and have her stop. Thank you for bringing this to our attention. I see you are calling from room 3421, Mrs. Susan — is that correct?

B: Yes, that's me. Thanks for taking care of this.

A: We want to make sure you have a good stay here, and you must be exhausted. Would you like me to tell the front desk to take phone messages for you this morning so you can rest for a couple more hours? We can also move your checkout time to 3 PM if you'd like.

B: Yes, that would help. Could you call me for a wake-up call at 13:30? I'll check out by 3 PM. That would be good. Thank you.

A: I would be happy to. Please call me if you need anything further. Again, my name is James.

B: Thank you, James, you've been great.

Dialogue 3

A: Good morning, madam. My name is Susan. I'm a room maid.
May I come in, please?

B: Yes. How long does it take to make up room?

A: It takes 20 minutes to make up your room, madam. Two of us will help to clean up everything in your room.

B: Can I stay in my room and watch television while you're working?

A: Certainly, Madam.

Dialogue 4

A: Good Morning, May I make up your room, please?

B: Are you a room attendant?

A: Yes, I'm a chamber maid. There are two of us help making up the room.

B: Would you come back in 15 minutes? I've not finished yet.

A: Certainly, Madam.
(15 minutes later)

A: Can I come in?

B: Yes, of course. We're leaving.

A: Goodbye Madam. Have a nice day.

B: Thank you.

UNIT 7

Hotel Doorman

7
UNIT

Hotel Doorman[11]

Dialogue 1

A: Good afternoon, sir. Welcome to Hills hotel. Can I help you with your baggage?

B: Thanks.
Take this suitcase, and I'll take my briefcase with me.

A: The front desk is through the doors, and to the right.

B: It looks like a nice place.

A: Is this your first visit?
I'm sure you will enjoy staying here.

B: Thank you.

11) a person whose job is to stand by the door of a hotel or public building and allow people to go in or out, and to open their car doors, etc.

Dialogue 2

A: Welcome to Hills hotel. How are you doing today?
B: Okay. How about you?
A: I am okay. Thank you.
Can I help you with your baggage?
B: That's all right. It's not heavy. I'll carry it by myself.
A: Have you ever been here before?
B: No. First time. Where do I register?
A: Register at the front desk over there to the right.
B: Thank you.
A: Watch out for the revolving door.
B: Thank you.
A: You're welcome.

Dialogue 3

A: Good morning, sir. Are you leaving today?
B: Yes.
A: Did you enjoy your stay here, sir?
B: Yes, I did.
My flight is at 2 o'clock. Could you get me a taxi, please?
A: Okay. I'll call a taxi for you.
B: How much does it cost to get to the airport?
A: About 30,000 won.
Here comes a taxi. I'll put your baggage in the trunk.
B: Thank you.
A: Have a good trip, sir.
B: Thank you. Have a nice day.

Dialogue 4

A: Good afternoon, Sir. Welcome to Lotte hotel. I hope you are having pleasant day so far. The reception is straight ahead, the lobby is on the right. Let me get the bellboy to assist you with your luggage.

B: Thank you.

A: Goodbye Sir/Madam. I hope you had a great time here at the Lotte hotel. Please join us again and enjoy your trip.

B: Thank you.

Dialogue 5

A: Good afternoon, sir, welcome to the Lotte hotel. may I help you with your luggage?

B: Sure thing. Thank you very much. Here it is···However I have to check in first.

A: No problem at all. The reception is over here. Please follow me.

----- After check in-----

A: Here is your room, sir. The keycard opens the door and switches on the electricity if you enter it here···. If you need anything, please do not hesitate to ask us at any time.

B: Thank you.

A: Do you need anything else?

B: Right now not, thank you.

A: My pleasure. Please enjoy your stay with us. Goodbye

Useful Expressions

- Good afternoon, sir.
- Welcome to Lotte Hotel
- We're happy to have you with us.
- How many bags, sir?
- It's five-minute walk.
- It's too far to walk.
- It takes fifteen minutes by taxi.
- It takes one and a half hours by bus.
- Shall I call a taxi for you, sir?
- I hope you enjoy staying with us.
- It'll be a pleasure to have you with us again.
- It should cost up to 10,000 won.
- Are these all of your luggage, sir?
- Where would you like to go, madam?
- Here is a map of the city to help you.
- Let me draw a map for you.
- It's within walking distance.
- Goodbye, sir. I hope you have a pleasant trip.
- Happy journey, sir.

UNIT 8

Hotel Bellman

8
UNIT

Hotel Bellman[12]

Dialogue 1

A: Good afternoon, sir. I'll show you to your room.
Do you have only one bag?

B: Hello. Yes.

A: After you, please. Is this your first trip to Seoul?

B: No. I've been here several times.

A: Is this the first time you've stayed at our hotel?[13]

---

12) attendant; bellboy; bellhop; tender; attender
someone employed as an errand boy and luggage carrier around hotels
Duties & Responsibilities:
- Greet guests in a friendly manner and offer assistance with luggage
- Operate the courtesy shuttle
- Baggage handling for tours
- Set up and break down of meeting rooms
- Communicate with other departments in a friendly and professional manner
- Be aware of local attractions and restaurants and make recommendations to guests
- Accurately communicate with other shifts regarding issues arising from day to day operations

B: Yeah. This is my first time. I've heard this is an excellent hotel.

A: I think so. I'm sure you'll agree after your stay.
This is your room 3114.
Enjoy your stay here.

B: Thank you.

Dialogue 2

B: Where can I park my car, sir?

A: You can park your car in the car park behind the hotel. It's free,

B: Thank you.

13) - Do you have any rooms available for (the seventeenth of April)?
- Is breakfast included?
- Does the room have air-conditioning?
- When can I check-in?
- Can I see the room, please?
- Can someone help me with my bags?
- Could I have a wake-up call at (seven o'clock), please?
- Is there an airport shuttle bus?
- When is check-out time?
- Could we please check-out a little late, at (one o'clock)?
- I'd like to book a room, please.
- I'd like a single room, please.
- I'd like a double room, please.
- The room is too noisy.
- I would like to change my room.
- We need (housekeeping service), please.
- We'd like to stay for an extra day.
- I've lost my room key.
- We're checking out now.
- We really enjoyed our stay.

Dialogue 3

B: I don't have a car and I'm not sure how I can get to the airport tomorrow morning.

A: There's no problem about transport to the airport. We have a courtesy coach to the airport that leaves every half-hour. It only takes 20 minutes to get there.

Dialogue 4

B: Is there a laundry service in the hotel?

A: Yes sir. Just leave your laundry bag behind the door with a laundry slip in it before 10 o'clock. Your laundry will be collected and returned to you by six o'clock in the evening.

Dialogue 5

A: Good afternoon, Mr. Cooper. Welcome to the Meridian Hotel.
Is this your baggage?

B: Yes, my stuff.

A: Certainly, please follow me. I'll take you to your room.

B: Thank you.

A: My name is James. It's my pleasure to serve you. If you have any questions, please feel free to ask.

(The elevator stops.) After you, Mr. James.

B: Thank you.

A: (In the hall way) This way, please. Here's your room 3451.
Where should I put your baggage, Mr. James?

B: Right on the bed.

A: Certainly, Mr. James. May I introduce the guest room facilities now?

B: Go ahead.

A: The minibar is right over there, beside the TV. The remote control is on the TV. The bedside console enables you to control the radio and the lights. There is an electric razor outlet in the bathroom, if you need it.

B: Is there any way I can get some more hangers?

A: Of course. Just dial 8 for Housekeeping.

B: Dial 8? OK, I've got it.

A: And there is a hotel brochure on the dresser. It includes a complete list of services and phone numbers.

B: Thank you for the information. I appreciate it.

A: You're welcome, Mr. James.

B: Thank you.

A: Have a nice day.

B: Thanks.

Useful Expressions

- Shall I call a taxi for you, sir?
- What is your destination, sir?
- Have a nice travel. Good bye.
- Good afternoon, sir. Let me take your baggage, sir.
- Please register at the front desk.
- Shall I load this suitcase into the taxi?
- Please proceed to the front desk.
- What's the plate number of your car?
- Good evening. Welcome to our hotel. May take your bag, sir?
- Sir, here is your key and please follow the bell man.
- Can you send someone to help me with my luggage?
- I locked myself out.
- I'd like to put some valuables in the hotel safe.
- What time does the dining room close?
- What time is breakfast served?

9
UNIT

Hotel Room Service

9

UNIT

Hotel Room Service[14]

Dialogue 1

A: Room service.

B: Good morning. This is room 2453. I'd like some breakfast, please.

A: Right. Excuse me. Mr. James?

B: That's right.

A: What can I do for you?

14) Continental Breakfast $25
Choice of two Breakfast Pastries or Muffins, Sliced Fruits, choice of individual Yogurt and Fresh Squeezed Juice, special blend Modern Honolulu French Press Coffee or Luxury Hot Tea
Omelet $18
Your choice of three toppings:
Cheddar, Swiss, Parmesan, Mozzarella, Bacon, Chicken-Apple Sausage, Portuguese Sausage, Ham, Spinach, Mushrooms, Tomato, Onion, Peppers, Asparagus
Additional toppings: $2 each
Rib Eye Steak $40
10 oz. Grilled Rib Eye, Whipped Potatoes, Asparagus, Sauteed Mushrooms, Bordelaise Sauce

B: I'd like some grapefruit juice, marmalade, two scrambled eggs with two sausages, toast, and a pot of black coffee, please. How long will it take?

A: Just a few minutes, sir.

B: Great. Thank you.

Dialogue 2

B: Good morning. This is room 1455. I'd like some breakfast, please.

A: Right. Excuse me. Mr. James?

B: That's right.

A: What can I do for you?

B: I'd like some orange juice, two scrambled eggs with two sausages, toast, and a pot of black coffee, please. How long will it take?

A: Just a few minutes, sir.

B: Great. Thank you.

Dialogue 3

B: Hello, This is James. How can I be of assistance?

A: I would like to order room service.

B: Certainly Sir, what is your room number and name, please?

A: It's room 1317 and the name is John.

B: Thank you. What would you like to order Mr. John?

A: I'd like New York Strip steak.

B: How would you like your steak cooked?

A: Well done, please.

B: Would you like mashed potatoes and vegetables or salad and fries?

A: Mashed potatoes and vegetables. Thank you.

B: Which sauce would you prefer?

A: I will have mushroom sauce.

B: Okay, is there anything else you'd like Mr. John?

A: I'd also like the garden salad and a coke.

B: Certainly Sir, that will be delivered to your room shortly. Enjoy your meal.

A: Thank you.

Dialogue 4

A: Room service, can I help you?

B: Good morning. Can I order some room service?

A: Of course, sir. What would you like?

B: I'd like a continental breakfast.

A: Very good, sir. Would you like tea or coffee?

B: Coffee. Could I have a cappuccino?

A: Certainly, sir.

B: How long will that be? I'm in a hurry this morning.

A: It'll be with you in ten minutes.

B: Good.

A: Could I have your room number, please?

B: It's 3512. Mr. James.

A: Thank you, Mr. James. Goodbye.

B: Thank you. Goodbye.

(About ten minutes later.)

A: (Knocks the door.)

B: One moment. Just coming!

A: Good morning, sir. Room service.

B: That was quick.

A: One continental breakfast with a cappuccino.
Could you sign here please, sir? Thank you. Enjoy your breakfast.

B: Thank you.

Useful Expressions

- The service was good, but not great.
- Now how much should we tip the maid for cleaning our room?
- I think a dollar a day is good enough.
- Only a dollar? I think two would be better.
- Let's see, we tipped the taxi driver 15% on the way to the hotel.
- He was very helpful, so it was worth it.
- And we tipped 12% at the restaurant.
- Come over to the window and look at the view.
- Wow! Look at the waves. I can't wait to go for a walk along the beach.
- Hey, this room is really nice! And big, too.
- Let's go out and enjoy the sun and sea now. We can unpack our suitcases later.
- That's a great idea. Grab a towel and some sunscreen and let's go!
- Will you be checking out now?

UNIT 10

Hotel restaurant

10

UNIT

Hotel restaurant[15]

Dialogue 1

A: We're looking for a good restaurant for dinner?

B: What kind of food are you interested in?

15) Asking about the menu
These are phrases you can ask the waiter if you aren't sure of something on the menu.
"What's … exactly?"
"Is this served with … (salad)?"
"Does this have any … (seafood) in it?"
"What do you recommend?"
Ordering
What the waiter says:
"Are you ready to order?"
"Can I take your order?"
"Anything to drink?"
"Would you like … (chips) with that?"
What the customer says:
"I'll have…"
"I'd like…"
"Can I have …"
"We'd like to order …"
If there are problems with the order, the waiter can say:
"I don't think we have any more … (lobster) left. I'll check with the kitchen."
"I'm sorry, but the king prawn soup is finished

A: Since we are in Korea, we want to try Korean food.

B: The Korean Restaurant is always a good choice.

A: Thank you very much. We'll try it.

Dialogue 2

A: I'd like to make a reservation for three people on Monday.

B: What time would you like?

A: 7:00.

B: We don't have anything available at 7:00. Is 8:10 ok?

A: Yes, that's fine.

B: Your name please?

A: James.

B: Ok, Mr. James. We'll see you at 8:10 on Monday.

A: Thank you. Bye.

B: Goodbye.

Dialogue 3

A: Can I help you?

B: A table for three please.

A: This way.

A: Are you ready to order?

B: Yes, we'll have the chicken with vegetables, and the vegetable pasta please.

A: Anything to drink?

B: Some water, coke, and sprite, please.

A: Can I get you anything else? Coffee? Dessert?

B: Coffee and Strawberry ice cream, please.

Dialogue 4

A: Hi. How are you doing this afternoon?

B: Fine, thank you. Can I see a menu, please?[16)]

A: Certainly, here you are.

B: Thank you. What's today's special?

A: Tonkatsu(Pork Cutlet) & Rice with honey bread.

B: That sounds good. I'll have that.

A: Would you like something to drink?

B: Yes, I'd like a coke.

A: Thank you. Here you are. Enjoy your meal!

B: Thank you.

A: Can I get you anything else?

B: No thanks. I'd like the check, please.

A: That'll be $25.50.

B: Here you are. Keep the change!

A: Thank you! Have a good day!

Dialogue 5

A: Good evening sir, welcome to Lotte House, can I help you?

---

16) Food equipment
- dinner fork/meat fork. dessert spoon
- dinner knife/meat knife. dessert fork
- soup spoon. water goblet
- butter knife. red wine glass
- salad fork. champagne flute
- salad knife. white wine glass
- fish fork. napkin
- fish knife. butter dish /milk jug /coffee pot
- bread basket/ sweet knife saucer
- dessert plate /jam dish/ napkin
- sugar bowl/ coffee cup

B: Can we have a table for four please.

A: Please come this way please.

A: Are you ready to order now?

B: Yes, we are. Can we have the Sunday roast with vegetables and Chicken salad please?

A: Would you like anything to drink with your meal?

B: 2 glasses of white wine, 1 coke, and 1 sprite, please.

A: Would you like to see the dessert menu

B: Okay, How about coffee? And can we have the bill please.

Dialogue 6[17)]

A: Hello, I will be your waitress today. Can I get you both any drinks?

B: Yes. I would like an iced coffee, please.

C: And I will have the same please.

A: OK 2 iced coffees, here you are. Are you now ready to order your, or would you like a few more minutes?

B: I think we are ready to order. I will have the chicken soup to start, and the steak with fries and the mixed vegetables.

A: How do you want the steak cooked rare, medium, or well done?

B: I would like it well done, please.

C: I do not want a starter. I would like to have the fried chicken with fries and a side salad please.

A: Your meals will be here shortly.

A: Here are your meals. If you need anything else just ask. Have a nice meal!

17) Italian dressing/Ranch dressing/Caesar dressing/French dressing/Thousand Island dressing/Balsamic vinaigrette/Raspberry vinaigrette/Honey mustard dressing
Red wine vinaigrette/Blue cheese dressing/Sesame ginger dressing/Russian dressing
Strawberry Poppyseed Vinagrette/Greek dressing/Western/Catalina Salad Dressing
Onion/Oil and Vinegar

Dialogue 7

A: Good morning. Could I have your room number, please?

B: Good morning. We're in Room 2341.

A: Thank you. The continental breakfast is on the buffet over there. Feel free to help yourselves. Here are your menus if you'd like something from the kitchen. I'll come and take your order in a moment. Can I bring you some tea or coffee?

B: Coffee for me, please, with hot milk.

C: And tea for me.

A: What kind of tea would you like?

C: American breakfast, please. With milk. And could we have some toast?

A: Of course. Would you like white, brown, or whole-wheat?

C: Brown-wheat, please.

A: Here's your tea and coffee, and your toast.
Would you like anything from the menu?

B: I'll have the sausages, scrambled eggs, and hash browns.

A: Sir?

C: I'd like the strawberry pancakes, please.

A: Thank you. I'll get those for you right now.

....

Here you are. Enjoy your breakfasts. Is there anything else I can get you?

C: No, thanks.

A: Thank you.

B: Thank you so much.

A: You're welcome.

C: Thank you very much.

Dialogue 8

A: Good evening, madam. Welcome to the Seoul restaurant.
May I take your coats?

B: Good evening. Thank you.

A: Would you like an aperitif before you order?

C: Yes, please. Two glasses of prosecco.

A: Let me give you some menus. I'll come back to take your order in a few moments.

B: That's wonderful, thank you.

A: Of course. We also have some specials on the board.

C: What are the specials?

A: The specials today are rack of lamb, lemon sole and a vegetarian pasta dish.
(Later)

A: Here you are. Two glasses of prosecco. Are you having wine this evening?

B: Thank you. Yes, we are.

A: Here's the wine list. We have three excellent red and white house wines and on the last pages you'll find the full wine list.

B: Thank you.

A: Let me know when you're ready to order.

B: Thank you so much.

A: You're welcome.

Dialogue 9

A: Are you ready to order, ma'am?

B: I think I'll have the French onion soup.

C: I'd like a beef consommé.

A: And what would you like for the main course?

B: Is there anything you recommend?

A: Of course, madam. Why don't you try our veggie steak?
It's very good.

B: What is veggie steak?

A: It's a vegetarian steak. Tofu is prepared as a steak and seasoned with salt, pepper, and garlic. We cook until it's crispy on the outside and hot in the middle. It's one of the chef's specials.

B: That sounds so nice. I'll have that.

A: And you, sir?

C: I'll have fillet mignon.

A: How would like it, sir?

C: Medium-rare, please.

A: Would you like a salad, ma'am?

B: I'll have a mixed salad.

A: And for you, sir?

C: A Caesar salad, please.

A: Would you like anything to drink with your meal?

C: We'll have two glasses of white wine, please.

A: All right, so that's the French onion soup, beef consommé, veggie steak, fillet mignon—medium, mixed salad, Caesar salad, and two glasses of white wine. Your order will be served shortly.

………………

(The diners have finished their main courses.)

A: Sorry to interrupt. May I clear away your plates?

C: Yes, please do. We've finished.

A: How were your main courses? Was everything satisfactory?

C: Yes, thank you. It was all excellent.

A: Would you like to see the dessert menu?

B: Yes, please. (Looks at the menu.)
I don't know what to have.
What would you recommend for the dessert?

A: I can recommend caramel custard, or you might like blueberry pie.

B: I'd like caramel custard. How about you, Chris?

C: No, thank you. I think I'll skip dessert.

A: Can I bring you anything else? A coffee or a digestif, perhaps?

C: Could I just have an espresso?

A: Of course.

C: And then could I have the bill, please?

A: Of course, sir. I'll be back right away with your caramel custard and coffee.

C: Can I pay by credit card?

A: Yes, sir. Oh, I'm afraid we don't accept that kind of credit card, sir. Only VISA.

C: OK. Then I'll use my VISA card.

A: Here's your bill, sir. Please put your card in the terminal, enter your PIN, and then press the green OK button.

C: All right.

A: Thank you, sir. I hope you enjoyed your dinner.

B: Thank you.

C: Thanks.

Useful Expressions

- Could I have chips (AE: French Fries) instead of salad?
- What can you recommend?
- Please bring me the bill (AE: check) with my coffee.
- I think you've made a mistake.
- A table for two, please.
- May we sit at this table?
- What's on the menu?
- May we sit at this table?
- We're not ready yet.
- Can you bring me the ketchup, please?
- I'll have the same.
- That's all, thank you.
- Can I have the bill (AE: check), please?
- This is on me.
- The rest is for you.
- Do you have wine by the glass?
- I'd prefer red wine.
- Please bring us another beer.
- Is everything all right?
- Did you enjoy your meal?
- Are you paying together?

- May I show you to a table?
- If you wait, there'll be a table for you free in a minute.
- Do you want vegetables with it?
- Why don't you try the pizza?
- It'll take about 20 minutes.
- Have you booked a table?
- How many are you?
- Would you follow me, please?
- Can I take your order, sir/madam?
- What would you like to start with?
- What would you like to drink?
- What would you like for dessert?
- How would you like your steak? (rare, medium, well done)
- Do you want a salad with it?
- What kind of dressing?
- Anything to drink?
- Do you want a dessert?

11
UNIT

Hotel Maid

11

UNIT

Hotel Maid[19]

Dialogue 1

A: We have to[19] check bedroom accessories. It contains linen Basket including sheets, pillow cases, bathrobes, lavatory Napkins, pajamas, bath and face towels, blankets, and dressing gown, spare pillow, and so on.

B: I'm cleaning the bathroom and checking these articles. There are shampoo bottles, foam bath, hair conditioner, toothpaste, tooth brush, sewing kits, candle stands, razor, sanitary bags, shower cap, body lotion, soap dish, detergent, first-aid box, ashtray, disposal bags laundry forms, laundry bags, room freshener, towels, facial paper, toilet paper, clothes hangers, breakfast knob cards, room service menu, waste paper basket, bath mats, bath towel, plastic shirt bags, polish my shoe card, Turkish towel or terry towel, a box of matches, blade

18) Hotel maids get little respect (or money) for their physically demanding work. We wanted to learn what their job is really like, beyond the "Do Not Disturb" signs and chocolates on pillows. Here are a dozen secrets about their duties, including the constant time crunch, the bizarre (and horrifying) things they have encountered in guest rooms, and the reason they suggest you don't use the hotel cups.

19) Business English for hotel staff, American English Conversation. 2016

dispensers, gargle tumblers, water tumbles, cotton pad. And I must also clean the shower curtain, toilet bowl, toilet flush, bath tub, and shower. Check the tap or faucet works well, and the plug sockets for shaving which are use for electricity of 220 volts, and even check that the toilet flushes properly.

A: I prepare sheets, blankets, bed spread. Pillow, mattress Protectors, Pillow cases for making beds.

B: On the writing table, must not forget to check the writing case containing writing paper. Envelops, facsimile form, a note pad, hotel guest comment form, guest house rules, brochures, post card, scribing pad, guest stationery, and ball point pens.

A: I'm putting the missing items in it. Even on the dressing-table, I put the hotel menu and guide book for the guests. In the drawer, there are a Bible and a book of Lord Buddha Preaching. In the wardrobe. You will see the coat hangers,

B: I will wipe the dust from the venetian blind, curtains, radiator, television set, air conditioner, easy chair, reading lamps, telephone, mirrors and the chair in the corridor.

A: Very good. Look in the mini bar, we always have some kinds of snacks for the guest. The refrigerator contains purified water, Spirits and soft drinks with tumblers, ice-cubes, napkins, a water jug or a carafe and the last thing is the price list.

B: When we finish checking the supplies, I will change the bed, and vacuum the rugs and draperies, supply stationery, change flowers when they are witted, check light bulbs, television set and hairs dries, clean the ashtrays and sweep the floor. We must also have and eye for details.

A: I have been trained to clean all types of room: single room, double room. twin room, studio room, penthouse suite, junior and presidential suites, duplex suite, double suite adjoining room and connecting room, exhibition room or display room, cabana and triple room.

B: Well, you must be an expert in cleaning.

A: Thank you, I'm sure I will be.

12
UNIT

Hotel Laundry

12

UNIT

Hotel Laundry

Dialogue 1

A: Hello. Can you please send someone to pick up my laundry from my room?

B: Sure. Would you like me to send the laundry staff right now or later?

A: Well, I'm leaving to go on a fishing trip in about 20 minutes. So, if you could send someone in the next fifteen to twenty minutes, that would be great.

B: Sure, Sir that won't be a problem.

B: What is your room number?

A: My room number is 1635.

A: When will the clothes be returned to my room? I'm leaving on Sunday.

B: Well, today is Friday, it usually takes a day so should be ready to collect tomorrow evening, but you can ask the laundry staff for a better estimate.

A: Alright I will do. Thank you.

B: You're welcome, sir.

Dialogue 2

A: Hello. You are the person who's in overall charge of the hotel?

B: That's right. But in fact the Assistant Manager is responsible for the day-to-day running of the hotel. You see, most of my time is taken up with negotiation with agencies, planning, meetings, that kind of thing.

A: I see. And then, under the Assistant Manager there are all the departments of the hotel.

B: Yes. You will find much the same departments in every hotel, but the actual details of organization always differ somewhat.
In our case we have three main divisions—the restaurant staff, the housekeeping staff and the reception staff. Reception is what the public see.
And in our case we have three receptionists who work under the Head Receptionist.

A: And do the porters come under reception too?

B: In this hotel, yes. Here, the Head Porter reports to the Head Receptionist. And the Head Porter in turn has two porters under him.

A: And housekeeping is a separate department?

B: That's right. The Head Housekeeper is in charge of the chambermaids and the cleaners.

A: What about the bars? Where do they fit in?

B: Well, we have four bar operatives looking after the bars in the hotel.
But the bars and the restaurant all come under the responsibility of the restaurant Manager. The restaurant section includes both restaurant and bar service.

A: OK. And under the restaurant manager you also have the waiters and the kitchen staff?

B: OK. As regards the waiters, the Head Waiter supervises three station waiters and a part-time waiter. And then there are the chefs. Under the Head Chef we have the Second Chef and two trainee chefs.
And there are several part-time kitchen assistants -the number varies.

A: Thank you very much for the information.

13
UNIT

Hotel Information Desk

13
UNIT

Hotel Information Desk

Dialogue 1

A: Good afternoon, sir.

B: Hello.

A: How may I help you?

B: Where can I buy some candies?

A: At the counter, over there.

B: Thanks. Would you recommend a place for shopping?

A: I'd like to recommend Dongdaemoon big shopping center.

B: I've heard of it before. How can I get there?

A: The tour desk can take care of you.

B: OK. Thanks.

A: It's my pleasure.

Dialogue 2

A: Good evening, sir.
B: What can I do for you?
A: Can I have some information about the night club?
B: It's located in the basement, and open from 9 p.m. till 3 in the morning.
A: That's great.
Would you recommend some place for dinner?
B: I suggest you have dinner at the Japanese restaurant on the 10th floor.
You'd better make a reservation.
A: Can you tell me the phone number?
B: Extension 312.
A: Thank you.
B: You're welcome. Have a nice day.

Dialogue 3

A: Hello. How are you today? How can I help you?
B: I am fine. Thanks.
I'd like to go to the Namdaemoon market.
Can you tell me how can I get there?
A: It's downtown. Wait a minute, please.
I'll draw a road map for you.
B: Thank you.
A: Here you are.
I wrote this one in Korean for you.
B: That sounds good.
A: Just show this one to the taxi driver.
And this is the hotel's card in case you need it on your way back.
B: Thank you. Do you know how much does it cost to get there?
A: I don't know exactly.
B: Thanks.

14
UNIT

Wake up call

14 UNIT

Wake up call[20]

Dialogue 1

A: Hello, I am James.

B: Yes, Sir. How may I help you today?

A: I have a plane to catch tomorrow morning and I can't miss it. Is it possible to arrange a wake-up call for 6:00am?[21]

---

20) Hello sir is very polite way of answering the telephone. The hotel receptionist could have answered hello John, but saying yes, sir is more professional.

21) • I'm sorry, we don't have any rooms available.
- Your room is on the second floor.
- Your room number is (901).
- Sorry, pets are not allowed.
- Sorry, smoking is not allowed.
- Please sign your name here.
- Here is your key.
- There is a restaurant on the ground floor.
- More fresh towels are available at the front desk.
- Thank you for staying with us!
- I'd like a room for 2 nights, please?

B: Yes, I am arranging that right now. What is your room number?

A: I am staying in room 1352.

B: OK, you'll get your wake-up call at 6:00 in the morning. Is there anything else I can help you with today?

A: Yes, I'd like to have some breakfast and a pot of coffee delivered to by room after my wake up call.

B: What breakfast would you like a full English or continental breakfast.

A: A full English with extra toast please.

B: Alright.

A: Yeah. That'll be all for now. I will settle my bill, when I check out in the morning.

B: Would also like me to arrange a taxi to the airport for you?

A: Hmm, yes that would be great. Can you order one for 7:00am.

B: Yes, that will be fine. Is that all?

A: Yes, Thanks for all your help.

B: It was my pleasure. Have a nice day.

A: Thanks.

Useful Expressions

- You will be in room 2352.
- I'd like to reserve(book) a room for one night.
- Your room is on the second floor.
- What's the room rate for a single room?
- Would you have a double room available?
- This is your key.
- Would you have a room available for three nights?

• Can I see the room, please?
• Do you have a room with a bath?
• What time is breakfast?
• Where's the restaurant?
• What time is check out?
• Are there any laundry facilities?

- Can I use the internet in my room?
- May I have your name and phone number?
- How much is a double room?
- Breakfast is included.
- How long will you be staying?
- The lift is on your left.
- Do you have any vacancies?
- I have a reservation under the name of James.
- Is breakfast included?
- We only have one single room left.
- How many nights will you be staying?
- Can you give us a discount?
- Can I book a room for tonight?
- I want 2nd floor.[22)]
- Do you have a reservation?
- What time is breakfast served?
- I'd like to check in. I have a reservation.
- Do I pay now or at checkout?
- I have a reservation for two nights.
- I have booked a double room for two nights.
- There is a safe deposit box in each room.
- Yes. We have a locked storage room.
- Can I leave my luggage here?
- I would like to check out.
- Can you prepare our bill?
- What time is checkout?
- We are looking forward to welcoming you again in our hotel.
- Can you bring us some more towels?

---

22) First(1st),Second(2nd), Third(3rd), Fourth(4th), Fifth(5th), Sixth(6th), Seventh(7th), Eighth(8th), Ninth(9th), Tenth(10th), Eleventh(11th), Twelfth(12th), Thirteenth(13th), Fourteenth(14th) Fifteenth(15th), Sixteenth(16th), Seventeenth(17th), Eighteenth(18th), Nineteenth(19th) Twentieth(20th), Twenty-first(21st), Twenty-second(22nd), Twenty-third(23rd) Twenty-forth(24th), Twenty-fifth(25th), Twenty-sixth(26th), Twenty-seventh(27th) Twenty-eighth(28th), Twenty-ninth(29th), Thirtieth(30th), Thirty-first(31st)

- I'm going to call the front desk.
- I'd like a wake-up call at 6:00, please.
- We'll unpack our suitcases later.
- May I have an extra pillow, please?
- May I have an extra blanket, please?
- Would you like me to call a taxi for you?
- Your food will be delivered promptly.
- Could you please call a taxi for us at 10?
- Late and early check ins can also be accommodated by arrangement.
- Room with private(shared) facilities.
- Guests may check in between 3 p.m and 9 p.m.
- Our hotel is suitable for families.
- Self-catering facilities are available.
- We can supply discounted tickets.
- We welcome caravans, motor homes and tents.
- Let's stop for lunch here.
- There's a picnic area.
- Let's pitch our ten here.
- We have a 24-hour reception and bar.
- Digital key card access is required for the bedrooms.
- Free wi-fi in social areas.

15
UNIT

Hotel Concierge for Sightseeing Advice

15

UNIT

Hotel Concierge for Sightseeing Advice

Dialogue 1

A: Good afternoon, sir.
The front desk told me to ask you for sightseeing advice.

B: Of course. I'd be more than happy to help. I am, after all, the hotel's concierge.

A: Concierge? What exactly is that?

B: We advise you on where to visit, eat, or shop during your stay here in Seoul.

A: Great! So where should I start my sightseeing?

B: The Kyungbuk palace is always a good place to begin.

A: I saw the Kyungbuk palace on my last visit here. Can you recommend somewhere else?

B: OK. What type of interests do you have?

A: In my spare time, I really like to view art and go shopping.

B: Have you been to Dongdaemoon or Insadong?

A: No, but I've heard a lot about both.

B: Well, Dongdaemoon is wonderful for shopping. Afterwards, you should head to the Museum to enjoy the art, Insadong.

A: OK. That sounds like a plan. Thanks.
B: I'm sure you'll have a good time there.
A: Thank you. Have fun.

Dialogue 2

A: Hello. How are you?
I was told to see you about going sightseeing.
B: I'm fine. Thank you.
It's my pleasure. I'm the hotel's concierge, at your service.
A: Concierge? Could you explain that to me?
B: We help direct hotel visitors to popular places to visit, eat, and shop.
A: OK. So where shall I begin my sightseeing?
B: I would suggest the Dongdaemoon.
A: Gee, I've already seen the Dongdaemoon. What about another site?
B: Let me see. What do you like to do in your spare time?
A: I really like to see the good place. And I like art.
B: Well, there you go! Have you ever visited either Namdaemoon or Insadong?
A: No, but I've been meaning to.
B: Well, Namdaemoon is fantastic for shopping. Then you can go to the Insadong.
A: That sounds like a great plan. I'll do that.
B: Enjoy your shopping and your visit.
A: Thank you.
B: You're welcome.

Dialogue 3

A: Hello. How's it going?
I need some sightseeing advice.
B: I'm fine. Thank you.

How about you?

That's what I'm here for, sir. Every good hotel has a concierge like me.

A: I don't travel a lot. What exactly is a concierge?

B: A concierge helps visitors like you find great places to visit, shop, and eat.

A: That's great! So tell me, where should I go first?

B: I'd suggest that you start at the Hong Ik University area.

A: You know, I've already been there. Can you suggest another place?

B: Maybe. Tell me what you like to do in your spare time.

A: When I have some free time, I often spend it watching movie or at museums.

B: Well, have you ever been to either Sam il Plaza or the Museum of ancient Art?

A: No, but I sure would like to.

B: Sam il plaza is great for just about watching movies. Then you can visit the Museum of ancient Art.

A: Both places sound great. I'll try to do that today.

B: Enjoy the views at both places.

A: Thank you, sir.

B: You're welcome.

Dialogue 4

A: Hi. How are you doing?

I'm going sightseeing, but I'd like to get your advice first.[23)]

23) Statements You Might Say

- I'd like to book a room, please.
- I'd like a single room, please.
- I'd like a double room, please.
- The room is too noisy.
- I would like to change my room.
- We need (housekeeping service), please.
- We'd like to stay for an extra day.
- I've lost my room key.

Questions You Might Hear

- Do you have a reservation?
- May I have your name, please?

• How long will you be staying?
• Could I see your I.D., please?
• How many guests are with you?
• Could you please fill out this form?
• Do you need help with your bags?
• Do you need a wake-up call?
• Are you familiar with [Vancouver]?
• Is there anything else we can help you with?

Statements You Might Hear
• I'm sorry, we don't have any rooms available.
• Your room is on the second floor.
• Your room number is (901).
• Sorry, pets are not allowed.
• Sorry, smoking is not allowed.
• Please sign your name here.
• Here is your key.
• There is a restaurant on the ground floor.
• More fresh towels are available at the front desk.
• Thank you for staying with us!

Visitors At The Front Desk
• I'd like a room for 2 nights, please?
• Can I see the room, please?
• Do you have a room with a bath?
• What time is breakfast?
• Where's the restaurant?
• What time is check out?
• Are there any laundry facilities?

Questions You Might Ask
• Do you have any rooms available for (the seventeenth of April)?
• Is breakfast included?
• Does the room have air-conditioning?
• When can I check-in?
• Can I see the room, please?
• Can someone help me with my bags?
• Could I have a wake-up call at (seven o'clock), please?
• Is there an airport shuttle bus?
• When is check-out time?
• Could we please check-out a little late, at (one o'clock)?

10 Statements You Might Say
1. I'd like to book a room, please.
2. I'd like a single room, please.
3. I'd like a double room, please.

B: I'm okay. Thanks. How about you?
I'm only too happy to help. Tourists should always check with their concierge first.

A: Concierge? I'm not familiar with that word.

B: A concierge directs visitors to the city's great tourist, shopping, and eating places.

A: That sounds great. Now, is there any place that I should hit first?

B: Well, if you're like most people, you'll want to go to the Sin chon.

A: I've already seen it, I loved it, but today I want to go somewhere else.

B: Sure! Tell me about your interests.

A: I like to just see the people and I like to see the works of the masters.

B: You'll get along fabulously at Han gang river and the Museum of ancient Art! Have you been to either?

A: No, I just haven't had the opportunity.

B: You'll love Han gang river for playing. Later on, you can go to the Museum of ancient Art.

A: Thank you. That's what I'll do.

B: This might be the best day of your visit.

A: Thank you very much.

B: You're welcome, sir.

Dialogue 5

A: Good afternoon, sir. How are you today?
I need some sightseeing advice. I was told to come to see you.

B: Hello. I am okay.
As your concierge, it is my pleasure to help you, sir.

---

4. The room is too noisy.
5. I would like to change my room.
6. We need (housekeeping service), please.
7. We'd like to stay for an extra day.
8. I've lost my room key.
9. We're checking out now.
10. We really enjoyed our stay.

A: Concierge? Are we speaking Korean here?

B: A concierge helps you find all the great places for visiting, shopping, and eating.

A: What would you suggest that I visit first?

B: How about starting at the Yongsan? Many people like to begin there.

A: The last time I was here, I visited the Yongsan. So do you have another place in mind?

B: I think so. Tell me what interests you.

A: I'm big on playing, although maybe I like art even more than playing.

B: Then you must go to Yeoido and Seoul National University. Have you been to either one?

A: No. I haven't had a chance to go to either of them.

B: Both places are usually crowded with tourists. You'll love the Yeoido and Seoul National University.

A: Thank you. That's great advice.

B: This might be the best day of your visit.

A: Thanks a lot. Have fun.

B: Thank you. Enjoy your trip.

Dialogue 6

A: Hello. How are you doing?
Can you give me some advice about going sightseeing?

B: Hi. I'm okay. How are you, sir?
Your concierge, sir, is the right person to ask when you need sightseeing advice.

A: Fine. Thanks. What in the world is a concierge?

B: We direct visitors to all the great tourist, shopping, and eating spots in the city.

A: Then what would you recommend as a starting point for my sightseeing?

B: Definitely the Lotte world. I think that is everyone's favorite first stop.

A: Actually, I've already been there twice. Do you have another suggestion?

B: I think I can come up with something. How do you spend your spare time?

A: I keep my mind active by visiting museums.

B: Well, the Museum of ancient Art and Everland were made for you! Have you gone to either one?

A: No, although I've heard great things about both of them.

B: You don't want to miss either place. The Everland and the Museum of ancient Art are big and beautiful.

A: Sounds great!

B: This is a day you're going to remember for a long time.

A: Thank you, sir.
Have a nice day.

B: Thanks a lot. Have fun.

16
UNIT

Hotel Amenities

16

UNIT

Hotel Amenities[24)]

Dialogue 1

A: Hello. How are you doing?
We're looking for a good restaurant for dinner?

B: I'm fine. How are you?
What kind of food do you prefer to eat?

A: Thanks. Since we are in Seoul, we want to try special cuisines from here.

B: The Royal Korean restaurant is always a great choice.

A: Thank you very much for the suggestion. We'll surely try it.

B: Thanks.

24) hotel amenities in english
Hotel room amenities
Kitchen facilities, like: fridge, coffee maker and microwave.
TV with cable.
Hair Dryer.
Essentially kit, like: soap, shampoo, body milk, conditioner, Towels.

Dialogue 2

A: Hello. How's it going?
I need to check my e-mail. Is there an Internet café near here?

B: I'm OK. Thanks. Absolutely, sir. The Business Center at the hotel has Internet access.

A: Can I also surf the Internet there? 25)

B: Of course sir.

A: Can I also save important files to a disk or flash memory?

B: Yes sir

A: Do you know how much they charge?

B: I'm sorry sir, but I'm not really sure of their rates. Although I'm sure it's a nominal fee.

A: Ok, thank you.

B: No worries sir.

Dialogue 3

A: Hello. How are you doing?
The office move, as you know, the plans have been up by the main exit for a week now. I just wanted to see what kind of feedback you've got.

B: I'm fine. How's it going with you?
I'm sorry, but I really strongly disagree with the new floor plan. I think It's divisive to separate the secretaries and the assistants out from the editors and managers. I'd be much happier if we could be located in teams.

---

25) Hotel facilities:
Restaurants Swimming pools
Café's, Tennis courts
Lounges Children's program
Spas Gym/Fitness Centers
Saunas Swimming pools
Steam rooms Conference rooms
Gift shops Business centers

C: Actually, I think James is right. I've been chatting to some of the secretaries and they're quite keen to all be sitting in the same area, and, speaking as an editor, I think I'd like to be with other editors so that we can bounce ideas off each other and things. So I think James's floor plan is right.

A: OK.

Dialogue 4

A: Hello. How are you doing?

First of all, the book re-launch. I just wanted to remind everybody that we will be re-launching the fairy-tales range with new modern covers, and that this is going to happen at the beginning of next month. It's important that we get this right and there have been quite a few···

B: I'm fine. How's it going with you?

Actually James, can I just ask you - sorry to hold the meeting up - can I ask you about those dates, because I thought that this was going to be published the month after next, and I understand that everybody has got their dates, but I do feel quite strongly that we're bringing this out too soon.

A: Well, any other thoughts before I comment on that?

C: I don't think we've got any choice at all about it. If the radio programmes are going out at the beginning of next month, we've got to launch the book at the same time if we're going to have any sales impact.

B: OK.

Dialogue 5

A: Hello. How are you doing?

James, can I have a word please, in my office? Now then. I won't take long about this, I'll come straight to the point. We had a chat...

B: I'm fine. How's it going with you?

A: At that point, I wasn't particularly happy with the way that you were behaving in the office, the way that you were being uncooperative, a little bit surly with people. And since then, frankly, I've seen very little change.

B: Well, I mean, I think I've made an effort, trying to be helpful like I normally am with people, and I feel that I'm still doing my job - not that the job's very interesting. I think it's become less interesting since Sarah got the promotion. I think she's getting some more of the interesting work.

A: Okay, well I'm afraid that, despite what you say, it hasn't come across. I don't want to jump to any conclusions, but you have taken quite a bit of time off … and …

B: Yes, but you're allowed to take leave, aren't you?

A: You are allowed to take leave. Hopefully you come back from leave refreshed and you leave your problems at home.

B: OK.

Dialogue 6

A: Hello. How are you doing?
Okay - any other business?

B: I'm fine. How's it going with you?
Yes, I would like to say something. An illustrator came in last week, and I think she's very good and it would be wise to put her on our books.

A: Okay.

C: I would like to be able to show her drawings and her portfolio in the next couple of days. If that's all right...

B: That sounds good.

A: Yes, I'll look forward to seeing those. Right, I think that's probably about It, but anybody got anything else that they desperately want to raise before we wrap up?

B: No.

A: No? Okay. We'll be having another meeting, but there are a couple of conflicts in the diary so I think the best thing is if I email the date of the next meeting.

B: OK.

Dialogue 7[26)]

A: Hello. How are you doing?
Welcome to Hills Hotel. May I help you?

B: I'm fine. How's it going with you?
I'd like a room please?

A: Would you like a single or a double?

B: I'd like a double, please?

A: May I have your name, please?

B: James.

A: Could you spell that please?

B: J-A-M-E-S

A: How many are in your party?

B: Just three.

A: How many nights would you like to stay?

---

26) - I would like to book a room.
- I'd like a single room.
- I'd like to book a double room for 3 nights.
- How much is a double room per night?
- I'd like a room with a nice view.
- Can I have an extra bed for my room?
- I'm arriving late. Please keep my reservation.
- When does the dining-room open?
- When is breakfast served?
- Where can I keep my valuables?
- I'd like to order room service, please.
- I would like to have a wake-up call at 5:30.
- What is the check-out time at this hotel?
- Do you have a bus service to and from the airport?
- Could you show me my room?
- Where is the elevator?
- Where is the emergency exit?
- The bed sheets are dirty.
- There's no hot water in my room.
- Where can I get some ice?
- The air-conditioner is not working.
- I'd like to check out.

B: Just two nights.

A: How will you be paying?

B: Is Visa OK?

A: That'll be fine. Would you like a wake-up call?

B: Yes, I'd like a wake-up call for 6:00. Do you have a pool?

A: Yes, we do. On the first floor. Here's your key. That's room 3451 on the sixth floor.

B: Thank you.

Dialogue 8

A: Hi, How are you doing?
My name is James and I have a reservation for tonight.

B: Thanks. I'm okay.
Let me check. OK, yes. A twin room for two nights.

A: That's right.

B: You are in room 3421. How would you like to pay for the room?

A: Do you take visa card?

B: Certainly, sir?

A: OK.

B: Yes. that comes to 765 dollars.

A: Do I pay now or when I check out.

B: In advance, please.

A: Here you go.

B: The elevator is just around the corner. Do you need any help with your bags?

A: No thanks. I can manage myself.

B: Is there anything else we can do to help you enjoy your stay?

A: Can you give me a wake-up call at 6:00?

B: We don't do that from here. You can use the clock radio in the room, or you can program the telephone in your room to ring at 6:00.

A: Oh, yes. I have a meeting downtown tomorrow. Does this hotel have a shuttle bus?

B: No, I'm sorry we don't, but we will be happy to call a taxi for you if you provide us with the details.

A: No, that won't be necessary. I can call from my room.

B: There are no charges for local calls.

A: Thank you.

B: You're welcome.

17
UNIT

A taxi in a hotel

17

UNIT

A taxi in a hotel

Dialogue 1

A: Hello, would you organize me a taxi for tomorrow morning?

B: That will be no problem. Where do you want the taxi to take you?

A: Well, I have to be at a business conference for 9 o'clock at the Lotte hotel. I'm hoping that it is not very far away from here.

B: That will be no problem. It's only a twenty minute drive from this hotel and your will be fine as the traffic is very quite at that time.

A: Then eight thirty will be fine. No! make it one fifteen to be on the safe side. Book the taxi for 8 am, please.

B: That will be no problem.
OK. I will make booking right away for you.

A: Thank you for your help. And please tell the taxi company to make sure the taxi arrives by 8 am, as that will leave me plenty of time.

B: That will be no problem.
Would you like me to order a taxi for when you return?

A: That's a great idea. Could make sure the taxi waiting for me outside for 11 o'clock.

B: That will be no problem.
Don't worry, we'll take care of that.

A: Thank you.

18
UNIT

Tourism

18

UNIT

Tourism

Dialogue 1

A: I need some sightseeing advice. I was told to come to see you.

B: As your concierge, it is my pleasure to help you, sir.

A: Concierge?

B: A concierge helps you find all the great places for visiting, shopping, and eating.

A: What would you suggest that I visit first?

B: How about starting at the Kyungbok palace? Many people like to begin there.

A: The last time I was here, I visited the Kyungbok palace. So do you have another place in mind?

B: I think so. Tell me what interests you.

A: I'm big on running, although maybe I like art even more than running.

B: Then you must go to Han river and the Museum of Korean Art! Have you been to either one?

A: No. I haven't had a chance to go to either of them.

B: Both places are usually crowded with natives and tourists. You'll love the Han river and the Museum of Korean Art.

A: Thank you. That's great advice.
B: This might be the best day of your visit.
A: Thank you.
B: You're welcome.

Dialogue 2

A: Hi. Are you okay? Where should we go sightseeing?
B: Yeah, I'm okay.
I think that some things might be best done in the afternoon and others in the evening.
A: I think that I would like to go to the Kyungbuk palace this afternoon.
B: That would be a good place to start our sightseeing. We could have lunch there.
A: I think there is a very good history museum there.
B: I think so, it would be good to check that out since we are so close by.
A: After that, where should we go in the evening?
B: I think that I would like to go to the amusement park-Lotte world. It's supposed to be quite nice.
A: At the end of the day, I would love to take in the sunset at the restaurant by the Lotte-world.
B: That sounds like a great idea! Let's go get a map.
A: OK.

Dialogue 3

A: Hello. How are you doing today? It's so hard to choose where to go first on our sightseeing trip.
B: I am good. A little bit tired. We could think of what would make a good afternoon activity versus morning activity.
A: I really wanted to make sure that I got a chance to go to the Han river.

B: I think that would be a fun beginning to our day. We could walk around there.

A: I heard that the History Museum is pretty close to the Han river.

B: I heard the same thing. We might as well go there since we are just down the street.

A: What would be a good place to go to in the evening?

B: The Namdaemoon market is supposed to be wonderful.

A: The restaurant on the edge of the Namdaemoon would be a great place to buy something good.

B: That sounds like a perfect sightseeing day to me.

A: It's a wonderful.
I like it. Let's go.

Dialogue 4

A: It's very hot today. Are you okay now? There are so many places to go on our sightseeing trip.

B: OK. I'm okay. Let's figure out what to do before dinner and later figure out what to do in the evening.

A: I heard that the Han river is a place that can't be missed.

B: That would be a relaxing way to begin our afternoon. It would be nice to get out in the sun.

A: The Dongdaemoon is close by, isn't it?

B: That Dongdaemoon market is supposed to be fantastic.

A: Do you have any suggestions as to where we could go in the evening?

B: We could check out the Dongdaemoon market.

A: We could eat dinner at the Dongdaemoon market.

B: That could really end up being a great day.

A: That's a great idea.

B: OK. Then let's go.

A: Okay. Let's go.

19
UNIT

Hotel Minibar

19

UNIT

Hotel Minibar[27]

Dialogue 1[28]

A: My minibar is completely empty.

B: Everything in that minibar has been consumed, sir?

A: Everything's gone.

27) A minibar is a small refrigerator, typically an absorption refrigerator, in a hotel room or cruise ship stateroom. The hotel staff fill it with drinks and snacks for the guest to purchase during their stay. It is stocked with a precise inventory of goods, with a price list. The guest is charged for goods consumed when checking out of the hotel. Some newer minibars use infrared or other automated methods of recording purchases. These detect the removal of an item, and charge the guest's credit card right away, even if the item is not consumed. This is done to prevent loss of product, theft and lost revenue.

28) -Are you ready to order?
- The soup of the day is "Cream of Broccoli."
- Our specials are listed on the board.
- I recommend the vegetarian chili.
- We can substitute the bacon for cheese, if you like. (=We can give you cheese instead of bacon)
- I'll be right back with your drinks.
- This meal consists of three courses - soup, the main course, and dessert.
- The chicken comes with your choice of rice or potatoes.
- I'm sorry, we're fully/completely booked (=we have no free tables) right now.
- If you would like, you can wait at the bar until a table opens up. (=becomes available)

B: Is there anything special you'd like?
A: Just bring me four bottles each of Cass beers and Hite beers.
B: Okay, sir. Four of each. Would you like anything else?
A: The fruit basket was great. I need a few more bananas, please.
B: Cass beers, Hite beers and bananas. Is that it for now?
A: Yes, one last thing: I could use some orange juice.
B: Your order will be brought to you momentarily, sir.

Dialogue 2

A: Hello. How are you?
I need someone to come up and restock the minibar in my room.
B: I'm fine. Thanks. How are you doing?
Does everything need to be restocked?
A: The good stuff needs to be restocked.
B: Tell me what's good to you, ma'am.
A: The four mini bottles of sparkling water were great.
B: OK.
A: I just need cass beer to go with ice.
B: Do any of the snacks need to be restocked?
A: Give me roasted nuts.
B: You like nuts, sir?
A: Yeah, I like it.
B: Okay, just give me your room number and someone will restock those items.
A: Room 3412.
B: OK.

Useful Expressions

- An Americano is a shot of espresso poured into a glass of hot water.
- Java is a very common slang word for "coffee."
- If you prefer, we can substitute the regular milk with soy milk.
- Our muffins are baked fresh every morning.
- All the tables inside are occupied, but our outside patio has plenty of free tables.
- All of our coffees are made from high- quality beans.
- Make sure you grind the coffee beans right before you brew the coffee.
- This is our most popular coffee = This is the coffee that we sell the most
- A cappuccino is a combination of coffee, steamed milk, and foam.
- Milk foam is commonly referred to as froth.

20
UNIT

Hotel Gym

20

UNIT

Hotel Gym

Dialogue 1

A: Do you have a swimming pool in this hotel?

B: We don't have a pool, sir, but we do have swim stations in the gym.

A: I never heard of a swim station. Is that like a bathtub?

B: Yes, it's just a deep bathtub with a current of water that you swim against.

A: I never heard of such a thing. How much do they cost?

B: As a guest, sir, you pay nothing.

A: This sounds better every second. Now, when can I use the stations?

B: If you want to swim, you can visit the gym any day between 6 a.m. and 9 p.m.

A: This is going to be great. I'm going to the gym right now!

B: I'm sure you'll enjoy your workout, sir. Everyone seems to like the swim stations.

A: Thank you.

B: You're welcome.

Dialogue 2

A: Hello. How are you doing?
Is there a gym in this hotel?

B: I'm fine. Thanks. How are you?
The fitness center is located on the fourth floor.

A: I'm OK. Thank you.
Is there a charge for me to use it?

B: No, it's free to all of our guests.

A: Very good. Can I go use it right now?

B: Unfortunately, the gym is only open from 6 a.m. to 8 p.m. and it's 9 p.m. now.

A: I guess I'll use it tomorrow then.

B: Just use your room key card to get in.

A: Are there weight machines?

B: The gym has weight machines, some treadmills, and some elliptical machines, too.

A: What about a personal trainer?

B: I am sorry. There are no personal trainers, just the machines.

A: OK. Thank you.

21
UNIT

(Hotel) Storing Luggage

21
UNIT

(Hotel) Storing Luggage[29)]

Dialogue 1

A: I'll be checking out of the hotel in about 20 minutes.
B: Twenty minutes and a few second, sir, it doesn't matter, I'm ready for you.
A: As you know, however, the day in Seoul has hardly begun.
B: There's nothing like getting an early start, sir.
A: What can I do with my baggage while I visit a few more tourist spots?
B: You can leave your baggage in our storage space, with a deposit.
A: Isn't my baggage enough of a deposit?
B: I wish it was, but it isn't. They will still want a credit card.
A: It's always something, isn't it? Let me think about this for a second.
B: Don't forget that you have very little time, sir, before you have to check out.

29) Dear Guest, Greetings from Hills Hotel. Thank you for your interest in our hotel. You may leave your luggage at our concierge on the day after checking-out from 13:00.
Please do not hesitate to contact us if we could be of any further assistance to you.
Thank you very much and we look forward to welcoming you at Hills Hotel.
With warm regards from the World's Best Hotel in Seoul's Most Exciting City.

A: Thank you.

Can You Leave Luggage at a Hotel Before Check-In?

Most larger hotels allow early luggage drop off. While some smaller establishments offer hotel luggage storage before check-in, it's always best to inquire about luggage storage when you book.

Do Hotels Hold Luggage after Check-out?

Larger hotels might allow you to store luggage at the hotel after check-out . But some hotels charge a fee to store luggage after check-out. You may be better off just booking an extra night.

Can I Store My Luggage at a Hotel Even if I'm Not a Guest?

Travelers often ask, "Will a hotel hold my luggage even if I'm not staying there?" The answer is usually "yes." Hotel bellhops will often agree to store your luggage for a tip. Keep in mind that this arrangement is informal. While hotel employees may be able to find a somewhat secure place to store your bags, busy bellhops won't be able to keep an eye on them constantly.

Can I Store My Luggage at the Airbnb?

When you're planning an early arrival, you should find out ASAP if early luggage drop-off is allowed at your Airbnb. If your Airbnb doesn't have an occupant booked after you, you may be able to store your luggage after check-out. Early Airbnb luggage drop-off is rarely available for high-turnover rentals.

Are There Any Alternatives to Hotel Luggage Storage?

Most hotels operate with a store-at-your-own-risk policy. Hotels may even require you to sign a waiver before storing your bags. And sometimes the luggage rooms in hotels look like they've been hit by the zombie apocalypse. A mountain of nearly identical bags sits piled on top of each other in a seemingly random fashion. The attendant is multitasking and can't properly keep an eye on the hotel luggage hold. It's not unusual for items to get damaged or lost. Occasionally, hotel guests even leave with the wrong bag by mistake.

Fortunately, these days travelers have alternatives to hotel luggage storage. Hills offers safe, affordable and convenient luggage storage at over 20 locations in more than 10 cities. For a small flat-fee per bag per day, you can store your luggage at one of Hill's secure Jang locations. Hills offers travelers a host of benefits, including:

Convenience- Online booking is fast and easy. You'll find Jang hosts near major tourist attractions and transportation centers. We've even partnered with Hotels. com. You can book Hills luggage storage directly from the Hotels.com concierge app.

Affordability- Hills charges a flat fee of $3 per item in Korea. There are no size restrictions or hidden charges. That's much cheaper than the tip you'll have to pay a bellhop.

Security- Hill's award-winning team personally vets each Jang host. We offer our customers free luggage insurance of $500 for each item that you store with us.

Trust- In 2021, Kyung gave Hills their coveted Gold Trusted Service Award. Jang maintains a 3.5/6 rating from nearly 5,000 customer reviews. Additionally, Jang has earned endorsements from the University of Seoul.

22
UNIT

Hotel Bar

22

UNIT

Hotel Bar

Dialogue 1

B: Hello. How are you doing?

A: Okay, I guess. How about you? Bartender, could I have a drink? What's taking so long?

B: Excuse me, sir. Yes, what can I get you?

A: I'd like a whiskey sour.

B: Certainly sir, I'll get that straight away.

A: What a day! My feet are aching! Where's an ashtray?

B: Here you go sir. Did you have a busy day?

A: Yes, I had to walk all over town to get to meetings. I'm exhausted.

B: I'm sorry to hear that, sir. Here's your drink. That should help.

A: That's what I needed. Much better. Do you have any snacks?

B: Certainly, here are some peanuts and some savory crackers, and a napkin.

A: Could I have a stir stick?

B: Coming up... Here you are.

A: I'm sorry to say this, but these snacks are awful.
B: I'm terribly sorry about that, sir. What seems to be the matter?
A: The peanuts are stale!
B: I apologize sir, I'll open a fresh can immediately.
A: Thanks. Sorry to be in such a bad mood.
B: That's quite alright. Can I get you another drink? This one's on the house.
A: That's kind of you. Yes, I'll have another whiskey sour.
B: Right away, sir. Do you have any preferences on the whiskey?
A: What's that bottle over there?
B: That's Dimple - aged 12 years.
A: That sounds good. I'd like to smoke...
B: Just a moment, here's an ashtray.

A: Thanks. So how long have you worked at this bar?
B: It's been about ten years now. I love this job...
A: Okay.

Dialogue 2

A: Hello. It's good. Here's to our new contract.
B: Hi. Great. Here, here.
A: A toast to James.[30)]
B: Cheers.
A: I'd like to make a toast to John. May he live long and prosper!
B: May he live long and prosper!
A: That's good.
B: It's nice.

30) Cheers!/Here's to your health./Bottoms up (informal, used with shots)
Prost/Salut (sometimes people use foreign expressions with the same meaning)
Here's mud in your eye./Here's to your health.
Down the hatch.

Dialogue 3

A: Hello. How are you doing?
Bartender, can I have a drink? What's taking so long?!

B: I'm okay. How are you? May I help you?

A: I'm fine. Thank you.
I'd like a whiskey sour.

B: OK. I'll get that straight away.

A: What a day! My feet are aching! Where's an ashtray?!

B: Here you go sir. Did you have a busy day?

A: Yes, I had to walk all over town to get to meetings. I'm exhausted.

B: I'm sorry to hear that, sir. Here's your drink. That should help.

A: (takes a long sip) That's what I needed. Much better. Do you have any snacks?

B: Certainly, here are some peanuts and some savory crackers, and a napkin.

A: Can I have a stir stick?

B: Coming up... Here you are.

A: Thank you. You know, I'm sorry to say this, but these snacks are awful.

B: I'm terribly sorry about that, sir. What seems to be the matter?

A: The peanuts are stale!

B: I apologize sir, I'll open a fresh can immediately.

A: Thank you. I am sorry to be in such a bad mood.

B: That's quite alright. Can I get you another drink? This one's on the house.

A: That's kind of you. Yes, I'll have another whiskey sour.

B: Right away, sir. Do you have any preferences on the whiskey?

A: What's that bottle over there?

B: That's Valentine's vodka, aged 30 years.

A: That sounds good. I'd also like to smoke. Is that possible?

B: OK. Go ahead. Smoking in the bar is okay.

A: How long have you worked at this bar?

B: It's been about two years now. I love the challenges of this job.

A: OK. Good.

23
UNIT

Hotel Information

23
UNIT

Hotel Information[31]

Dialogue 1

A: Excuse me, can I have a local map?
B: Yes, here you are.
A: I want to have a city tour, do you have any suggestion?
B: You can go to the Han River or Yeoido.
A: How can I get there?
B: You can take city bus route 488 from our hotel to the Han River.
A: How can I go to Yeoido?
B: First, you can take Subway to Han river, and then take the bus to Yeoido.
A: What can I do over there?
B: You can watch the famous sunset and taste delicious seafood over there.
A: Sounds great. We should go there, thank you.

31) Reservation, Reception/front desk, Concierge, Bellboy/porter, Lobby, Amenities/facilities Guest, Room service, Wake up call, Housekeeper, Single (room), Twin (room), Double (room) Ensuite (bathroom), Clean, Complimentary, Tidy, Register, Call, Check In, Tip

Dialogue 2

A: What is that thing on the wall in the bathroom next to the shower?
B: It's the water heater?
A: How does it work?
B: Water passes through pipes heated by electricity to make the water hot.
A: How do use it?
B: First, press the lever at the bottom of the unit to turn it on. Then, turn the temperature setting dial to the temperature desired. After that, just turn on the water.
A: Does it take long to heat the water?
B: It takes only a couple of seconds.
A: What is this?
B: It is the remote control for the TV.
A: What does it do?
B: It can be used to control the TV, to turn it on or off, to change channels, and to adjust the volume. With this device you don't have to get up from your chair or bed to use the TV.
A: How does it work?
B: It operates on batteries and sends a signal from the remote to sensors in the TV that control the different functions.
A: How convenient!

Dialogue 3

A: Information. This is James speaking.
B: Hello. I'd like some information about having a wedding banquet at your hotel.
A: Certainly, sir. May I ask your name, please?
B: It's Susan.
A: What date you like to host the wedding banquet on?
B: May 6th.
A: Certainly. How many people do you expect to attend?

B: I think there will be 100 guests. So, I'll need 25 tables.

A: We have a room available, Ms. Susan. It fits 20 to 25 tables?

B: Great. What are our menu options?

A: We have three menus at $120, $150, and $200 per table.

B: OK. One more thing-- and what if some of our guests are vegetarians?

A: That will not be a problem, Ms. Susan. Would you like to come in and work out the details?

B: Sure. How about friday afternoon at around 4.00 p.m.?

A: Very well, Ms. Susan. We'll be expecting you this friday at 4:00 p.m.?

B: Thank you. See you then.

A: Thanks much.

B: You're welcome.

24
UNIT

Hotel Lost & Found

24
UNIT

Hotel Lost & Found

Dialogue 1

A: Good morning madam. May I help you?

B: Yes please. Please! I lost my purse!

A: Do you remember where you lost it or where you had it the last time?

B: This morning, during breakfast, I still had it. But in the afternoon I tried to pay for my poodle's hairdresser and couldn't find it.

A: Well don't worry, madam. We will check every inch of the hotel to find it. However, if we won't be successful we will, of course, assist you in getting substitute credit cards and everything you need.

B: Thank you so much. I'm really worried right now.

A: Don't worry ma'am, everything will be fine.

B: Thank you.

25
UNIT

Hotel Guest's Complaints

25 UNIT

Hotel Guest's Complaints

Dialogue 1

A: Why is our order taking so long?

B: Well sir, you ordered the steak very well done and it takes a little longer.

A:There are not enough towels in my room.

B: I'll have housekeeping deliver more towels to your room right away sir.

32) - Could I have another order of garlic toast?
- Yes sir, I'll take care of that right away.
- I would like extra soap and shampoo left in the room.
- I'll attend to that immediately.
- Would it be possible to get a two minute boiled egg?
- Of course sir, I'll be back with that item in a few minutes.
- Could you arrange a tee time of 6:30 AM for four at the Paradise Club?
- Of course sir, what is the name of your party.
- The guests in the next room are very noisy. Could we change rooms?
- I'm not sure, let me talk to my supervisor. I'll be back in a moment.
- Is it possible to get free samples of all the facial products the spa sells?
- Certainly ma'am, which products would you like?

A: The sink is leaking in the bathroom.

B: Sorry for the inconvenience, maintenance will be by shorty to fix the problem.

A: This soup is not warm enough.

B: I apologize for that ma'am. I'll have the chef warm it up immediately.

A: This tread mill doesn't seem to be working properly.

B: I'm sorry miss, why don't you used that one over there.

A: I seem to have misplaced my tennis racket. Has one been turned in?

B: Not yet sir, but I'll let you know if someone does. What is your room number?

A: I specifically requested an ocean view, but the room I was given has a view of the pool.

B: I'm sorry about the mix up sir, we'll change your room immediately.

26
UNIT

Hotel Facilities and Amenities

26
UNIT

Hotel Facilities and Amenities

Dialogue 1

A: Excuse me. We're looking for a good restaurant for dinner?
B: What kind of food are you interested in?
A: Since we are in Korea, we want to try Korean food.
B: The Korean Restaurant is always a good choice.
A: Thank you very much. We'll try it.
A: Could you recommend a place to take our kids? They're getting bored at the beach.
B: There's a movie theater in Seoul Town at Central Festival they might enjoy.
A: Well maybe. Is there anything else more exciting?

---

33) Restaurants, Shopping Malls, Cafés, Scuba diving,
Lounges, Snorkeling, Spas, Golf, Saunas, Island Tours
Steam Rooms, Boat Charters, Gift Shops, Elephant Treks
Gym/Fitness Centers, Zoos, Conference Rooms, Museums
Business Centers, Panoramic Vistas, Swimming pools, Aquariums
Squash Courts, Sea Kayaking, Tennis Courts, Open Traditional Markets
Putting/chipping greens, Nature treks, Children's Programs, Grocery Stores

B: Lots of kids seem to have a great time at the Go-Cart track.

A: No way. That's way too dangerous.

B: Have they ever ridden an elephant?

A: No, but is it safe?

B: Oh, absolutely. The elephants are well trained and the trainer leads the elephant along the path. Riders are strapped into the seats with safety belts, just like in a car. And to be truthful, the rides are not that long-45 minutes or so.

A: That sounds OK.

A: I need to check my e-mail. Is there an Internet café near here?

B: Certainly, sir. The Business Center at the hotel has Internet access.

A: Can I also surf the Internet there? I need to find some information for a meeting.

B: Absolutely sir.

A: Can I also save information to a disk or flash memory?

B: Of course.

A: Do you know what it cost?

B: To be honest sir, I don't really know. But I'm sure it's a nominal fee.

A: Ok, thank you.

B: My pleasure, sir.

27
UNIT

Hotel Jobs

27

UNIT

Hotel Jobs

Dialogue 1

A: What do you do?[34]

---

34) • I'm sorry, I couldn't write earlier because I was ill.
- Thanks for the letter and the wonderful photos of your hometown.
- It was interesting to hear about school life in Britain.
- I attend the "name of the school".
- It's a "type of school".
- How much homework do you get every day?
- In your letter you asked me to tell you something about schools in Saxony.
- There are 15 boys and 12 girls in my class.
- My friends and I don't get very good marks.
- We like jokes better than school.
- I studied for the English test all evening.
- How are you and how are you enjoying your job?
- Tell me about your working hours, your pay and your holidays.
- I'm going to start an apprenticeship as a mechanic on August 1st.
- It's very difficult to get an interesting job here.
- In September I have to start work.

B: I'm a events coordinator for a hotel?

A: What exactly does an events coordinator do?

B: Well, we arrange and set up all the things needed for a conventions and conferences for various groups. We try to ensure that every thing runs smoothly and efficiently during the event.

A: That's sounds interesting.

B: It has its moments.

A: What's your job?

B: I'm a chef.

A: Are you a head chef?

B: Well, I'm the head pastry chef.

A: Sounds sweet. Where do you work?

B: At the Lotte Arcadia Spa and Resort.

A: What do you do for a living?

B: I'm employed at a hotel as a bell man.

A: So you take people's luggage to their rooms.

B: Yes that, but I also arrange things like taxis for guests. One of my most important functions is to be a source of information. I provide a lot of information to guests, such as the kinds of facilities and their location in the hotel, places to eat in the area, and places to go and see on the island.

A: Just out of curiosity- do guests tip well?

B: Some do, some don't.

- I have made up my mind to become a nurse.
- I can write good stories when I feel like it.
- I don't like school very much.
- I'm planning to visit Wales next year.
- Now I have to finish this letter.
- The sun is shining and therefore we want to go swimming.
- I'm looking forward to getting your letter.

28
UNIT

Travel English at the Airport

28

UNIT

Travel English at the Airport

Dialogue 1

A: Good morning! Where are you flying to today?[35)]

B: Seoul Korea.

A: May I have your passport, please?

---

35) • Instead of "Where are you flying today?" the agent may ask "What's your final destination?" The answer will be the same!

• You can say "Here you go" anytime you give something to somebody

• To check your bags means to put them on the airplane inside the cargo compartment. The small bag you take with you on the airplane is called a carry-on. You need to put your carry-on bags through the X-ray machine at security.

• The scales the equipment that tells you the weight of your luggage

• A stopover or layover is when the airplane stops in a different city before continuing to the final destination

• If the agent says that your luggage will go straight through, it means it will go directly to the final destination (and you don't need to pick it up during your stopover)

• Boarding passes are the tickets that permit you to enter the airplane

• When a plane begins boarding, it means that the passengers start to enter the plane. Usually boarding time is 30-60 minutes before takeoff (when the plane leaves)

B: Here you go.

A: Are you checking any bags?

B: Just this one.

A: OK, please place your bag on the scale.

B: I have a stopover in Tokyo - do I need to pick up my luggage there?

A: No, it'll go straight through to Seoul. Here are your boarding passes - your flight leaves from gate 65C and it'll begin boarding at 11:00. Your seat number is 36D.

B: Thank you.

A: You're welcome. Have a nice trip.

Dialogue 2[36)]

A: Please lay your bags flat on the conveyor belt, and use the bins for small objects.

B: Do I need to take my laptop out of the bag?

A: Yes, you do. Take off your hat and your shoes, too.

(He walks through the metal detector)

---

36) • "Excuse me, where is the American Airlines check-in desk?"

• "How many bags can I check?"

• "Will my luggage go straight through, or do I need to pick it up in [Seoul]?"

• "How much is the fee?"

If your bag is heavier than the weight limits, or if your bag is larger than the size limits, you may need to pay extra: an oversized baggage fee or overweight baggage fee (this can be $95 to $450). Some airlines in the United States also charge a fee for ALL checked bags (usually $25 to $45).

• "Please mark this bag as 'fragile.'

Say this if you have fragile or sensitive items in your bag that might break

• "Is the flight on time?"

The agent will respond either "Yes" if the flight is on time, or "There's a 40-minute delay" (for example) if the flight will leave later than expected.

• Did you pack your bags yourself?

• Has your luggage been in your possession at all times?

• Are you aware of the regulations regarding liquids in your carry-on?

(Liquids must be 100 mL or less, and stored in a single quart-sized clear plastic bag)

• Are you carrying any firearms or flammable materials?

• Have you left your luggage unattended at any time?

• Has anyone given you anything to carry on the flight?

A: Please step back. Do you have anything in your pockets – keys, cell phone, loose change?

B: I don't think so. Let me try taking off my belt.

A: Okay, come on through.

(He goes through the metal detector again)

A: You're all set! Have a nice flight.

Dialogue 3[37)]

A: Sir? Would you like chicken or pasta?

B: I'll have the pasta.

A: Anything to drink?

B: What kind of soda do you have?

A: Coke, Diet Coke, Sprite, Orange, and Dr. Pepper.

B: Diet Coke, please.

A: Here you go.

B: Thank you.

Dialogue 4

A: Excuse me. Can you please help me find the counter of Air Korea?

B: Sure Sir, It is on the left hand side at counter no.30, beside the counter of Delta Airlines.

A: Thank you.

(At Air Korea counter)

37) • Can I have a pillow?
- Can I have a blanket?
- Can I have a pair of headphones?
- Could I have some water/coffee/tea?
- Could I have some extra napkins?

B: How many people are you? Can I have your passports and tickets?

A: We are three of us, here are our tickets and passports.

B: Thank you, please allow me a minute for verification. How much luggage do you have?

A: We have 3 bags for check-in and 2 hand baggage.

B: That's fine. Kindly put your check-in baggage on the conveyor belt. Also, please tie the baggage tags against all your handbags.

A: Sure, I will do that.

B: Sir, I believe you have exceeded your luggage's weight limit.

A: Oh! How many kg over are we?

B: The limit is 20 kg per person on check-in baggage and 7 kg on hand baggage. For three people, the limit would be 60 kg and 15 kg respectively. Your check-in baggage is 80 Kg sir.

A: So, what do you advise us to do?

B: You can take some time and rearrange your luggage over there sir, or pay fine which is 50 dollars per kg.

A: OK then. I would like to rearrange my luggage.

B: Right sir.

After 5 minutes

A: There you are sir, All done

B: Very well sir. Kindly put your luggage on the conveyor belt.

A: OK.

B: Fine sir. Here is your boarding pass and baggage tags are behind your boarding pass. Your boarding time is 15:30 pm at gate no. 34. Have a good flight. Thank you for choosing Air Korea.

A: Thank you so much. Have a good trip.

B: Thank you.

29
UNIT

Hotel Shopping

29
UNIT

Hotel Shopping

Dialogue 1

A: Welcome to Lotte boutique. How may I help you?
B: I'm looking for a bathing suit?
A: A one piece, two piece, or a bikini?
B: A two piece, but not too revealing.
A: We have some over here.
B: That blue and white polka dot one looks nice. How much is it?
A: It's $85.
B: That's a bit pricey, but I'll take it.
A: Good afternoon, may I be of assistance?
B: Yes, how much is the carved elephant?
A: That's $99.
B: Could you tell me what it's made from?
A: That's made from teak.
B: I'll take it.

B: Excuse me, do you have any yellow T-shirts?

A: Yes sir, they are right over there.

B: Thanks. Do you have any bigger ones?

A: Let me check in the back. I'll return in a moment.

B: Thanks.

A: Good afternoon, may I be of assistance?

B: No thanks, just looking around.

A: OK, if you need anything, just let me know.

B: Oh, I will.

30
UNIT

Walk in the same directions

30

UNIT

Walk in the same directions[38]

Dialogue 1

A: Could you tell me how to get to the Fitness club?

B: Take this passage-way and go down the steps on your right. At the bottom of the steps there is a wooden bridge. Go over the bridge and turn right. Follow the path until you get to the Fitness club? It's about 50 meters from the bridge.

A: How do I find the Korean Biwon restaurant?

38) Giving directions:
Take this passageway, Go up/down the steps, On your right/left, Turn right/left
Take the elevator, It's on the third floor
Follow this path, Turn right/left at the corridor
It's about 40 meters, Go above 2 kilometers
Cross the street, It's on your right/left
It's in the middle of the block./It's on the corner.
Drive south on 345./It's next to/across from/between/in front of
Drive to Jackson street and turn left/right

B: Just follow the pathway to the left of the reception desk in the Lotte lobby. The walk-way will take you directly to the Korean Biwon restaurant.

A: Which way do I go to get to the swimming pool?

B: From the Bell Desk in the Lotte Lobby, turn left and follow the path on the right and go past the pond and up the steps. From there, walk straight across the lotte road, the swimming pool will be right in front of you.

A: Pardon me, I'm lost, how do I get to the gym?

B: From the main lobby, walk away from the night club and take the first staircase on your right down. The staircase is next to the portrait center. The gym is on your right at the bottom of the stairs.

A: Which is the best route to the Hong In Moon?

B: Get on the road to Chongro and drive north on the 342. At the end of the lotte road in Dongdaemoon Gu, turn right on the 434 and drive east. Take the 23 about 3 kilometers and turn right on the 3521. That road will take you to Hong In Moon.

31
UNIT

Hotel telephone

31

UNIT

Hotel telephone

Dialogue 1

A: VIP Lounge. How can I help you?

B: Yes, this is Mr. James in room 1640. I'd like to arrange an horse ride for my daughter.

A: Certainly ma'am. When would you like to go?

B: How about 11:00 AM?

A: Would you also like me to arrange transportation to and from the ride?

B: That would be great, if it's not too much trouble.

A: No trouble at all ma'am. If you could meet me in the VIP Lounge at 11:00 I'll escort you to the taxi.

B: Sounds great. I'll see you then.

A: See you at 11:00 Goodbye.

A: Room Service, how can I help you?

B: Yes, could you send up a BLT, a bag of chips, and an ice tea.

A: Of course sir, could I have your room number?

B: It's 1321.

A: OK, your order will be there in about 20 minutes.

B: Thank you, goodbye.

A: Housekeeping, how can I be of assistance?

B: Could I have a couple more blankets sent up to my room please.

A: Of course ma'am. Could I have your room number.

B: I'm in room 1732.

A: They will be there in 5 minutes.

B: Thanks. Bye.

A: You're welcome, have a good night.

A: May I speak to Mr. James please?

B: He is not in at the moment. Can I take a message?

A: Yes, could you tell him that John called.

B: Could I have your number please?

A: Yes, it's 010-3419-3981.

B: I'll give him the message.

A: Thanks, bye.

B: Is this the James room?

A: Yes, it is.

B: May I speak to Mr. James?

A: He's not here, he's at the pool. Call I have him call you back?

B: Yes please, have him call the front desk. It's about the change in his departure flight.

A: I'll give him the message.

B: Thanks, bye.

<Message 1- A is calling, B is taking message>

Information for A Information for B

Name of caller: James Reason can't answer: Out of office

Name of person wanted: John

Reason for call: Meeting canceled

Message: Reschedule for Friday at 09:30

Message Memo

Date: ____________________________

Time:____________________________

To: ______________________________

Message: ____

____

____

<Message 2- A is calling, B is taking a message>

Information for A Information for B

Name of caller: James Reason can't answer: On another line

Name of person wanted: John

Reason for call: company merger

Message: Call office ASAP

Message Memo

Date: ____________________________

Time:____________________________

To: ______________________________

Message: ____

____

____

32
UNIT

Asking for Help

32

UNIT

Asking for Help

<When offering help>

A: Excuse me ma'am, Could I help you with your bags?

B: That would be great thanks.

A: Pardon me sir, but it likes you could use some help with those packages.

B: I sure could, thanks.

<When responding to help>

B: Excuse me, but can you help me?

A: Of course ma'am, what can I do for you?

B: Someone just stole my purse off my shoulder outside the hotel.

A: Are you OK?

B: Yes, just shaken up a bit.

A: Why don't you sit down here and I'll call the police for you.
B: Thank you; I appreciate your help.

B: I don't understand what the taxi driver is trying to say. Could you translate for me?
A: Of course sir, I'd be delighted to help.

33
UNIT

Hotel Checking in and out

33

UNIT

Hotel Checking in and out[39]

Dialogue 1

A: Hello, how may I help you?

B: Yes, do you have any room available?

A: Yes sir, we have mountain-view rooms and suites.

B: I'd like a room please. How much is it?

A: For one person the rate is $250 per night?

B: OK, I'll be staying for 3 nights. Could I see your driver's license please and please complete this form.[40]

39) 11am or 12pm check out and The 3pm or 4pm check in allows sufficient time for housekeeping to turn rooms over and clean them very good. If the hotel was sold out or someone threw a party and trashed the room, there's extra time to clean rooms so that by check in time your room is cleaned as if no ones been in it.

40) -Do you like staying in hotels?
- Have you ever stayed in a hotel?
- How often do you stay in hotels?
- Are there many hotels in your city?
- What are some famous beach hotels in your country?

B: Here you go.

A: Here is your room key. You'll be in room 1208. Do you need any help with you luggage?

B: No thanks, I can manage. Thank you.

A: Welcome to the Lotte hotel. How can I help you?

B: I'd like to check in. I have a reservation.

A: Of course, could I have your name please?

B: James.

A: Here you are. You are staying for 3 nights is that correct?

B: Yes, I may have to stay another day or two. Will that be a problem?

A: No problem sir. How will you be paying, with cash or a credit card?

B: I'll be using my Visa Card.

A: Could you complete this form and may I get a copy of your passport port?

B: Of course, here you go.

- What do you think about hotel food?
- What activities do you usually do in a hotel?
- What can you do in a hotel to have fun?
- Do you ever worry for your belongings when you stay in a hotel?
- What do you take into consideration when choosing a hotel?
- When was the last time you stayed in a hotel?
- Would you like to work in a hotel?
- What are three things that you like about staying in hotels
- What's your best hotel experience?
- Would you like to open your own hotel?
- Do you use room service?
- What do you think about Airbnb?
- Have you ever used Airbnb to find a place to stay?
- Do you drink a lot when you stay in a hotel?
- Do you eat a lot when you stay in a hotel?
- What do you think about working out in a gym hotel?
- What do you think about hotel charging an extra fee for using the hotel WIFI?
- What's your favourite hotel?
- Is there a hotel that you would never stay at again? Why not?
- What is your favourite service provided by the hotel staff?
- What are the necessities every hotel should have for a guest?
- What is the craziest thing you've seen at a hotel?
- Have you ever had an issue with your room or service and dealing with customer service?
- What are your thoughts about pets in hotels?

A: You are in room 1253. Here is your room key. I'll call a bell boy to assist with your luggage.

B: Thanks.

A: Have a pleasant stay.

B: I'm sure I will.

Dialogue 2

B: I'd like to check out please.

A: Of course, could I have your room number and room key?

B: Here you go.

A: Give me a moment to get the final bill. You used the mini bar, is that correct?

B: Yes, I had a couple of cokes and a bag of chips.

A: Here's the final bill. Will be still be paying by credit card?

B: Yes, here my Visa card.

A: Thank you sir. I hope you enjoyed your stay.

B: I did, thank you.

B: I want to check out please.

A: Yes sir, could I have your room number and key?

B: Room 1476. Here's the key

A: Did you use the mini bar sir?

B: No.

A: Here is the final bar. You'll be playing by cash, correct.

B: Yes, that's correct.

A: Here's you receipt and change.

B: Thanks, what time does the shuttle bus leave for the airport?

A: It leaves in ten minutes. You can board to the right of the front door.

B: Thanks, goodbye.

A: Good bye sir. Have a pleasant flight.

Dialogue 3

A: Hi. How are you doing?
I have a reservation for tonight.

B: I'm okay. How's it going? And your name?

A: I'm fine thanks. It's James.

B: Okay. Mr. James. That's a room for five, and . . .

A: Excuse me? You mean a room for five dollars? I didn't know the special was so good.

B: No, According to our records, a room for three guests was booked under your name.

A: No. Hold on. There must be some mistake.

B: Okay. Let's check this again. Okay, Mr. James B. James for tonight ...

A: Ah. There's the problem. My name is James Kim, not James B.
[Uhh] You must have two guests under the name.

B: Okay. Let me check this again. Oh. Okay. Here we are.

A: Yeah.

B: A room for one for the 25th ...

A: Wait, wait! It was for tonight. Not tomorrow night.

B: Hum. Hum. I don't think we have any rooms for tonight. There's a convention going on in town, and uh, let's see. Yeah, no rooms.

A: Ah come on! You must have something. Anything.

B: Well. We do have some rooms under renovation with just a roll-a-way bed. [U-hh] None of the normal amenities like a TV or working shower or toilet.

A: Ah man. Come on. There must be something else.

B: Well. Let, let me check my computer here. Ah!

A: What?

B: There has been a cancellation for this evening. A honeymoon suite is now available.

A: Great. I'll take it.

B: But I'll have to charge you 357 dollars for the night.

A: Ah. Man. I should get a discount for the inconvenience.

B: Well. The best I can give you is a ten percent discount plus a ticket for a free continental breakfast.

A: Hey. Isn't the breakfast free anyway?

B: Well, only on weekends.

A: I want to talk to the manager.

B: Wait, wait, wait Mr. James. I think I can give you an additional 15 percent discount and I'll throw in a free room for the next time you visit us.

A: That'll be a long time.

B: Thank you.

Dialogue 4

A: Good morning. How are you doing?
Welcome to Hills Hotel. How may I help you?

B: I'm okay. How's it going? My name is James. I have a reservation for a single room for two nights.

A: Alright, Mr. James. Let me pull up your reservation. I can't seem to find a record of your booking. Did you book the room directly through us, or did you use a hotel reservation service or a travel agent?

B: I booked it directly through you. I've already also paid a deposit on the first night. I have a reservation number if that helps.

A: Yes, sure. Can I see that please? Thank you. Oh, I see. Maybe there was a glitch with the booking system. Well, we don't have any more single rooms available, with the exception of one adjoined room. But, you would then be right next door to a family with children, which might get noisy. But that's not a problem. I can upgrade you to one of our business suites.

B: Oh! That sounds good. But how much more is that going to cost?

A: That would of course be at no extra charge to you.

B: Oh, thank you.

A: My pleasure.

B: What about the wireless internet?

A: Oh. It's really easy. This is your access code and instructions on how to use it. If you have any problems, feel free to call the front desk. And this is a list of all the hotel amenities, like the gym and the indoor pool.

B: Ah. Thank you very much.

A: You're welcome. Has the valet already taken your car or will you be needing a parking pass?

B: Oh. I don't have a car. I took a taxi from the airport.

A: Alright. Can I have some form of ID please? And could you just fill out this registration form?

B: Sure. Here's my driver's license.

A: Thank you. Oh, you're from LA.

B: Yes, I am. All the way from the west coast!

A: I hope you had a good trip.

B: Yes. I did, thank you. The flight was long but it was smooth and I slept almost the whole way.

A: And is this your first time in Seoul?

B: Yes, it is. I have a business conference to attend, but I'm looking forward to getting some sightseeing done as well.

A: Well, I'd be more than happy to give you some sightseeing tips if you need any.

B: Thank you.

A: Alright. I've got you all checked in to your room. This is your room key. You're in room 3421. Just take the elevator on the right up to the 13th floor. When you get off the elevator, turn right. Your room is at the end of the corridor on the left-hand side. Just leave your suitcase here and the bell boy will bring it up.

B: Great. Thank you very much.

A: If you need anything please feel free to dial the front desk. Enjoy your stay.

B: Thank you.

A: You're welcome.

Dialogue 5

A: Hello. How are you?
This visit is over for me. Here's your room key.

B: I'm okay. How's it going?
Thank you for that, and in return, here's your receipt.

A: And thanks to you.

B: I hope you'll visit us again, sir.

A: I'd be willing to try this hotel again, if you can promise me no more cockroaches.

B: I will try it. I hope your trip home is pleasant.

Dialogue 6

A: Hello. How are you? I'm leaving. Here is my key.

B: I'm okay. How's it going?
Just one second, sir, and I'll give you your receipt. Here you go.

A: Thank you very much.

B: Sir, did you enjoy your stay here?

A: Most of my time here was pleasant. And Seoul itself is fantastic.

B: I'm glad you enjoyed the city, anyway. But please don't think too unkindly of us.

A: OK.

34
UNIT

Hotel Bill Settlement

34

UNIT

Hotel Bill Settlement

Dialogue 1

A: Could I have the check please?

B: Of course sir, I'll be back in a moment.

A: I'd like to check out please.

B: Of course sir, could I have your room number and room key?

A: The room was 1743. Here's the key.

B: Did you use the mini bar sir?

A: Yes, I had a couple of sodas.

B: The total comes to $677. Will you be charging this sir?

A: Yes, put it on my Visa Card.

B: Sign here please. And thank you for staying with us.

A: There you go. Thanks

B: How will you be settling your bill sir?

A: I'll be paying by cash.

B: Yes sir, here's the bill.

A: Excuse me, but what is this charge for?

B: Let me see, it's for an apple pie.

A: But we didn't order apple pie.

B: I'm terrible sorry for the error sir. Let me refigure this. Here you go sir.

A: That looks right. Thank you.

B: Sorry for the error sir, and please come again.

B: Would you like to pay for the tennis court in cash or charge it to your room?

A: Just charge it to my room please.

B: Yes sir, if you could just sign here.

A: There you are.

B: Thank you sir, have a pleasant day.

35
UNIT

Hotel Valet Parking

35

UNIT

Hotel Valet Parking

Dialogue 1

A: (knock the door 5x) Valet service please.[42)]

B: Coming please.

A: Good morning Mr. James. I'm Tom from valet section. I would like to deliver your laundry. Would you like to check your laundry Mr. James?

B: Yes. it's good. may I know how much I must pay?

41) For Five Star, Five Diamond hotel valet service, look no further than Hills Parking. We design custom hotel valet programs, from guest arrival and first impression to check-in and room presentation. Our professional, polished staff really do make the difference. Each highly-trained Hills Parking valet is dedicated to and passionate about providing the distinguished service your guests expect. With high-profile clients like The Ritz-Carlton and Shilla Hotel & Spa, Hills Parking provides the experience needed to set your hotel apart.

42) Valet parking is a parking service offered by some restaurants, stores, and other businesses. In contrast to "self-parking", where customers find a parking space on their own, customers' vehicles are parked for them by a person called a valet. This service either requires a fee to be paid by the customer or is offered free of charge by the establishment.

A: Well Mr. James. I would like to explain to you about your laundry bill. The charge for 5 + 15 tax and service is 3. Due to you want emergency service, the additional charge for it is 10% from your amount. So, the grand total is 35.

B: Alright.

A: Excuse me Mr. James, Could I have you signature over here please?

B: Sure. (sign the bill)

A: Thank you so much Mr. James. Is there anything else?

B: No. thank you.

A: Well. thank you so much for your trust and interest Mr. James. If you need any further assistance, don't be hesitate to call us by dial number 0 to laundry service.

B: Thank you for your service.

A: With my pleasure Mr. James, have a nice day.

Dialogue 2

A: (Knock the door 3 times) Good afternoon, valet service.

B: (opens the door)

A: Good afternoon, I'm James from Housekeeping department valet section. You have requested for valet service, I'm here to pick up your laundry, may I come in?

B: Yes. please take it. it's behind the bathroom door.

A: Certainly Ma'am have you fill up the laundry request form.

B: Yes here it is.

A: Could I counter check your laundry first?

B: Yes please.

A: Well Ma'am. You have 3 shirts and 3 pair of trousers. The total is 6 pcs. Is that correct?

B: Yes.

A: Based on your laundry request form, you preferred your clothes to be machine Wash with liquid detergent to be used, the type of service is regular. Which means you have to wait for 12hrs before you receive your clothes dry and fold.

B: Yes I'm willing to wait.

A: Thank you.

Dialogue 3

A: Hello. How are you?
What is the best place to park?

B: I'm fine. How's it going?
What vehicle do you bring to this hotel? Is it an automobile or a motorbike?

A: I'm okay. Thanks. I drive a automobile.

B: OK. That means you can park in the regular parking lot or on the street. Have you seen the handicapped spots?

A: I am not sure what a handicapped spot is.

B: Look for the blue signs and blue marked spaces. Do you usually park in the daytime or the evening?

A: I park days and evenings.

B: Be careful about the time limits on the streets. Have you seen the signs for time limits?

A: What signs?

B: As long as you are careful reading the signs, you will always know how long you can park and what days are OK to park there. Are you aware of the curb colors?

A: What curb colors?

B: If you can remember that red means absolutely no parking and white means that you can only load and unload, you are going to be OK.

A: OK.

Dialogue 4

A: Could you tell me the time please?

B: It's 15 after two.

A: What's today's date?

B: It's May 5th.

A: What time is check out?

B: Check out is at 12:00 PM.

B: Good afternoon sir. How can I help you?

A: I would like to schedule a tennis game.

B: Certainly, what day and time would you like that for?

A: Do you have time available on Monday morning? About 10:00.

B: I'm sorry, we don't have any openings at 10:00, but there is time between 8:00 and 10:00.

A: How about 09:30.

B: Yes sir, could I have your name please.

A: It's James, room 1425.

B: OK Mr. James, we have you scheduled for Monday at 09:30. See you then.

A: Thanks you, bye.

Dialogue 5[43)]

A: What time do the local shops usually open?

B: They usually open between 9:00 and 10:00.

A: Do they usually open at the same time on Saturdays and Sundays as well?

B: Yes, most of the shops open at the same time on the weekends.

----

43) Hotel English is polite and formal.
Imagine a beautiful hotel lobby, where the receptionist at the desk greets you like this:
"Welcome to our hotel. How may I be of assistance today?"
Now imagine the same situation, only the words spoken by the receptionist are:
"Hey there, how's it going? You need something?"
It's not quite the same, is it? Working in a hotel means using more polite language than you would in your everyday life. It doesn't matter if you're speaking to an important businessman or a tourist on vacation. Everybody visiting the hotel is treated with the same high level of respect and formality.

A: When do Korean people usually eat dinner?

B: Most people eat dinner between 6 and 7 PM.

A: Is lunch usually between noon and 1:00 PM or between 1:00 and 2:00.

B: Lunch is usually between noon and 1:00.

A: How often do they change movies at the local cinema?

B: Movies are usually changed once a week.

A: Do they show a lot of English language movies?

B: Many of the movies are the latest Hollywood block busters, which are captioned in Korea.

A: How many times a week does the hotel clean the pool?

B: The pool is cleaned every day, sometimes twice a day, depending on the circumstances.

A: What time are they usually cleaned.

B: Usually early in the morning, before the guests wake up.

Dialogue 6

A: Good evening. How may I help you?

B: Do you have any rooms?

A: Yes. Single, double or twin?

B: Single, please.

A: Would you like a room with a shower or a bath?

B: Just a shower will do.

A: Room 1429. That'll be $345 a night, including breakfast. How long will you be staying?

B: Just a couple of nights. What time is breakfast?

A: Breakfast is from 06:30 to 09:00.

B: And what time is dinner?

A: Dinner's from 5:30 to 8:30. You'd better hurry, the restaurant closes in 30 minutes.

B: Thanks.

36
UNIT

Asking for allowance

36
UNIT

Asking for allowance[44]

Dialogue 1

A: May I pour you more wine, sir?

B: Sure.

----

44) DIALOGUE:
For my lower level students:
Can I move your card? Yes, you can.
May I move your card? Yes, you may.
For my middle level students:
Is it ok if I move your card? Yes, it is ok.
Do you mind if I move your card? No, I don't mind.
Would it be okay if I move your card? Yes, it would be ok.
For my more advanced level students:
Would it be alright if I moved your card? Sure, it'd be alright or Of course, it'd be alright.
Would you mind if I moved your card? No, I wouldn't mind.
If you don't mind, I'd like to move your card. Sure, I don't mind.
Would it bother you if I moved your card over there? No, it wouldn't bother me at all.
Is it alright to move your card so I can pick up my card? Sure, it's alright.

A: Do you mind if I clean the room now, sir?
B: Actually, would it be possible for you to come back in half an hour?
A: No problem, sir.

B: May I borrow your pen.
A: Absolutely sir, here you go.

B: Would it be a problem if I left my luggage here for a few minutes?
A: No problem at all, sir. I'll keep on eye on it.

A: Is it OK if I make a copy of your passport?
B: Sure, whatever you need.

37
UNIT

Hotel Compliments

37

UNIT

Hotel Compliments

Dialogue 1

A: What a beautiful dress, Ms. Susan.

B: Thanks, I'm glad you like it.

A: Your new hair-do looks absolutely gorgeous, Mrs. Esther.

B: How kind of you to say so.

B: My compliments to the chef. This linguine is superb.

A: Thank you ma'am. I'll be sure to let the chef know.

B: Your English is very good.

A: Thank you very much.

A: Excellent game Mr. James. You really gave me a workout.

B: Thanks, I guess all those private lessons are finally paying off.

B: I really appreciate all the extra work you did on helping us solve that problem. It truly went above and beyond. My compliments to your work ethic.

A: Thank you sir, how kind of you to say so.

38
UNIT

Hotel Questions

38
UNIT

Hotel Questions[45]

Dialogue 1

- Do you have free internet in the hotel?

Through the Link@Sheraton, guests may browse the Internet, watch a game with friends, borrow a magazine or newspaper, or have a cup of coffee at Starbucks. We offer wireless and wired internet for a fee in guest rooms. Guests can connect up to three devices for the cost of $10.35 for 24 hours. Club Level guests and SPG Members receive complimentary internet.

- Do you have a swimming pool/gym?

Yes, all guests may access the indoor/outdoor salt water pool and a state-of-the-art fitness center located on the 5th floor.

- What are the dining options in the hotel?

We offer several on-property Boston Back Bay restaurants.

45) Sheraton Hotel in USA

- **Do you have free breakfast?**

Breakfast is not included in most room rates.

- **Can I have something sent to the hotel before I arrive?**

All incoming packages and faxes are handled through our business center, FedEx, which is located on our second floor. Handling fees apply to all incoming and outgoing items. For fee information please visit Sheraton Boston shipping

- **How do I get to the Sheraton Boston Hotel from Logan Airport?**

You can take a taxi, public transportation or the Back Bay Logan Express, our Boston hotel airport shuttle. Please visit Sheraton Boston directions for detailed instructions on how to navigate to our hotel.

- **Do you have a free hotel shuttle to places in the city?**

Although we do not offer a free shuttle around the city, tickets for Old Towne Trolley Tours are available. See our Concierge staff for more information.

- **Where is the nearest subway station to the Sheraton Boston Hotel?**

The two nearest subway stations are the Green Line stations of Prudential station and Hynes Convention Center station. For a detailed map of the MBTA "T" and directions to points of interest around the city visit Boston public transportation map.

- **How much does it cost to park at the hotel?**

Sheraton Boston parking is available for $45 per night until 3:00 PM on the day of checkout. This valet parking fee includes unlimited in and out privileges. Guests can also park at the Prudential Center Garage for $43 for each 24 hour period. Please note that payment for this parking is separate from the hotel and you will be expected to pay each time you exit the garage.

- **What is the clearance on your garage/valet parking?**

The clearance in our garage is 6 feet. Our valet offers to take oversize vehicles on a space available basis; the rate for oversized vehicles is $342 per night.

- Where can I rent a car?

Right in our lobby - a fully-staffed Hertz car rental desk is located adjacent to our gift-shop. The direct dial number is 213-369-5846.

- What can I do within walking distance of the hotel?

The Back Bay neighborhood has long been one of the most exciting parts of town, and home to plenty of things to do in Boston.

- What are the recommended tours of Boston?

There are many great tours around Boston. Some of our highly recommended tours are Old Towne Trolley Tours

- The Boston Duck Tour
- Urban Adventures Bike Tour
- Boston by Foot Walking Tours
- Don Quiojote Tours (Spanish language tours of Boston)

- What is good to do with children in Boston?

Boston has many great places and things to explore with children. We suggest going to the Boston Children's Museum, exploring the Museum of Science, taking a Boston Duck Tour, seeing the penguins at The New England Aquarium, taking a ride on the Codzilla, walking to Fenway Park, riding a Swan Boat (seasonal), shopping at Faneuil Hall or heading over to the Skywalk at Prudential Center.

- Where can I go running nearby the hotel?

There are several routes around the beautiful Charles River. There is the option of a brisk 3.5 mile run or an extended 6 mile run.

- How far is Faneuil Hall?

Faneuil Hall is located about two miles from our hotel. It is easily accessible by subway and taxi cab. Faneuil Hall is known for its historic restaurants, including the famous Cheers, as well as the beginning of the Freedom Trail Tour.

- Can you recommend any restaurants nearby the hotel?

Please email the concierge desk and it will be our pleasure to email you a list of restaurants within walking distance of our hotel.

39
UNIT

Hotel Reception

39 UNIT

Hotel Reception

Dialogue 1

A: Good afternoon. Can I get a room in the Lotte Hotel please?

B: Have you made a Advance booking, Sir?

A: I'm afraid I haven't done any room reservation. I tried to do hotel online booking. I believe that hotel reservation software was not working then

B: What kind of a room do you want, Sir? A double room or a single room?

A: A single room, please.

B: Let me see. (Looking at the register). We are fully booked up at this time of the year. No, we haven't a single room available, sir.

A: But please do try to help me out. I wouldn't know where else to stay.

B: Would you like to see the hotel Manager, Sir? He just might have some rooms reserved for emergencies.

A: Thank you. Can you direct me to the Hotel Manager, Please.

B: I'll trace him for you in the hotel. Just a moment, Sir. (Talking into the phone). Please get me the Hotel Manager. He might be in booking office or he might have gone on a round of the hotel. It he is not in the booking office, try the Korean Restaurant. Thank you

A: In the mean while, can someone get my baggage out of the taxi?

B: Why not. Of course. (Tapping a bell for the porter. To the porter.) Please get the gentleman's bags out of the taxi. (To James) please do sit down. I'll speak to the Manager of the Hotel about a room for you, Sir.

A: What is the room tariff in this hotel

B: We charge $350 a day for a single room Sir.(The telephone rings.). Yes, I want to speak to the Hotel Manager. I am speaking from Hotel Reception. Good afternoon. Sir. I have a small problem. There is a guest here who has just arrived from Delhi. He wants a single room and we haven't any single rooms vacant. Is there some way of helping him out, Sir?

C: Just a moment. I'll come down myself.

A: (Approaching the hotel reception desk again). Could you get me a single room?

B: The Hotel Manager is coming down here and then we'll see what can be done. Don't worry, Sir. We'll try our best to help you out.

C: Good morning, Sir. I am the Hotel Manager. What is the problem?

B: The gentleman here has no reservation but requires a single room. All the rooms are booked up.

C: (Looking at the register). How long do you want to stay, Sir?

A: Just for one night. I'm catching the afternoon train tomorrow.

C: All right. I think we can accommodate you. Miss Susan, give the gentleman one of the room booked for the German group. Their plane has been delayed and they will now be coming in tomorrow by lunch time. Will that be all right, Sir?

A: Thank you very much.

C: You are welcome.

B: Here you sir, Sir. I am giving you a single room on the second floor. Will you please fill in your name and address in the registration book please Thank you.

A: Does the room rent include meals also?

B: No, Sir. Meals are charged separately. Here is your room key. We've put you in room 1356. The porter will take you bags up to your room. Is there anything else you would like, Sir?

A: No. Thank you very much.

B: It is a pleasure, Sir.

D: This way, Sir.

A: Oh yes, for got to mention. Can I get morning tea at 6 o'clock tomorrow morning?

B: Certainly Sir. We'll call you at 6 o'clock tomorrow morning, with tea. If you want to eat your meals in the hotel, you can either call Room Service, or come down to eat in one of the restaurants.

A: Thank you.

Dialogue 2

A: Thanks for meeting with me during your dinner hour.
I appreciate it.

B: No problem. I'm happy to help. What's going on?

A: Oh you know, the usual. Should I take this new job?
Or do I stick with my current one?

B: Well, I think it's time for a change, don't you?
They pay you late and you are unhappy.

A: Do you really think so?

B: I know so. And I've been listening to you complain for over a year now.
Trust me. Take the job. What do you have to lose?

40
UNIT

Hotel Greeting Guests

40
UNIT

Hotel Greeting Guests[46]

- **IF GOOD**
  How are you? Great.
  How's it going? Couldn't be better.
  How has your day been? Fantastic.

- **IF SO-SO**
  How have you been? Could be worse.
  How's the family? Fair to middling.
  Did you have a good day? I can't complain.

- **IF BAD**
  How do you feel? Not too good.
  How was your day? I've had better days.
  Have you had a good day? No, it was lousy.

---

46) More Formal expressions
Goodbye./Thank you for coming./Have a pleasant day.
Goodbye,/please come again./Goodbye, I hope to see you again.
Less Formal Goodbyes
See you later (soon)./So long/Good bye (bye) Please come again
I have to run I have to be going now./Catch you later/See you again

Dialogue 1

A: Good afternoon, welcome to The Lotte.
B: Hi.
A: How can I help you today?
B: I need to check in.
A: Of course sir, My name is James and I'll be your guest representative during your stay. Could I have your name please?
B: Thomas.
A: Yes Mr. Thomas, here you are. And how are you today?
B: Tired actually, it was a very long flight.
A: Well, I'll get you checked in as soon as possible so you can relax.

Dialogue 2

A: How do you like the weather on the island?
B: It's very hot, much hotter than I expected.
A: So, what's the weather like now in your country?
B: It's cold and snowy.

Dialogue 3

A: (seeing a guest with numerous shopping bags): Did you have a good time shopping?
B: Yes, I spent all morning in Dongdaemoon.
A: Were you buying souvenirs for the folks back home?
B: That, and a few personal items.

Dialogue 4

A: Please be very careful with that bag, there are fragile items inside.
B: Not to worry sir, I'll be extremely careful.

A: Is it possible to fix the drip in the sink. It keeps me awake at night.
B: I'll take a look at it right away sir. It probable just needs a new washer.

A: Instead of herbal tea, do you happen to have Earl Grey?
B: I'm sorry ma'am, but the herbal tea is all we have at the moment.

A: Could you fill out the form for me. I hurt my writing hand?
B: Of course sir. First, how do you spell your family name?

A: Could I get more weights added to this machine. This is no challenge at all.
B: I'll get more weight right away. How much more would you like?

A: Is it possible to get another pillow. This one smells funny.
B: Of course ma'am, I'm very sorry. I'll bring you a new one as soon as I finish up with the room, if that's OK.
A: Thank will be fine, thank you.

A: Could I get fresh pineapples finely diced mixed in with the pancake batter?
B: Of course sir, as you like.

A: Could I get a free sample of these products?
B: Which products would you like samples of?

A: How about all of them?
B: We don't have samples for all of the products, but you can have the samples we have.

41
UNIT

Hotel Complaints

41

UNIT

Hotel Complaints

Dialogue 1

A: Yes, this is James in room 2341. I have a problem with my laptop. I can't seem to connect to the Internet. It's very important. I'm really in a bind. I've got this wedding tomorrow, and I need to check the registry.

B: I'm very sorry for your inconvenience, Mr. James. Please allow me to call Tom. He's our maintenance engineer. He's pretty good with computers.

(A few minutes later)

C: At our hotels we need to dial 5 to get an outside line. So you need to go to your pull-down menu here and add a default to your user profile choices and ··· (Computer: "You've got mail.") There! You're on. Good to go.

A: Great. Thank you!

(Later)

B: Hi, Mr. James, this is Jane calling from the front desk. Yes, I was calling to make sure your Internet connection was working well.

A: The connection is fine, but the wedding registry is closed. I guess that's what I get for waiting until the last possible second.

B: That's too bad, but maybe there's something else we can do to help.

<Front Desk Staff>

A: When I first arrived I was assured that a bottle of Dimple would always be in the mini-bar. Well I''m here now and the bottle isn't. What kind of hotel are you running here anyway?

B: I sincerely apologize for the oversight sir. We have been exceedingly busy today because of the convention. I'll have a complimentary bottle delivered immediately. Please accept it with our compliments.

A: Well, I should hope it would be complimentary. Thank you. Good bye.

<Health and Leisure Staff>

A: I had a scheduled tennis game, but the court has been taken over by someone else.

B: Yes sir, I understand. But we have a policy that if a party is more than 15 minutes late for a starting time, we schedule the courts for other waiting guests. I'm terribly sorry, would you like to reschedule?

<Housekeeping Staff>

A: We ran out of toilet paper. Is it possible to get more?

B: I'm very sorry. Of course, ma'am. I''ll send more up immediately. Is there any thing else you require?

A: Now that you mention it, could you also bring up a six pack of Case?

B: Yes sir, I'll call room service immediately and have them send some to your room.

A: That would be great, thanks.

<Kitchen Staff>

A: I requested the eggs over hard, these are over easy.

A: Sorry about that sir, let me make you some more right away.

<Spa Staff>

A: Ouch! Are you trying to kill me!

B: I'm terribly sorry sir. Am I pressing too hard?

A: Yes.

B: How's this? Is this better?

A: It still hurts a little.

B: How about now? Is this OK?

A: Yes, that's much better. Thank you.

B: Again, I'm sorry sir. Please let me know if you have any other problems sir and I'll adjust my technique as you wish.

42
UNIT

Hotel Compliments 1

42

UNIT

Hotel Compliments 1

<Bell Desk Staff>

A: Your English is very good. You must study a lot.

B: Thank you sir. Yes, I study every chance I get.

B: This luggage is very unusual- strong yet light weight. I like it.

A: Thanks, it cost me an arm and a leg.

<Engineering/Maintenance Staff>

A: That was fixed very quickly. You must be very good at your job.

B: Thank you sir, I try.

B: Thank you for letting us know of this problem so quickly sir. Most quests would have waited until check out, if then.

A: My pleasure.

<Food and Beverage Staff>

A: What a lovely uniform, so colorful.

B: Thank you ma'am. How kind of you to say so.

B: Your patience regarding the delay is a true virtue sir. Many guests would have complained.

A: I understand: it's busy and hectic in here.

<Front Desk Staff>

A: I really appreciate all the extra work you did on helping us solve that problem. It truly went above and beyond; my compliments to your work ethic.

B: Thank you sir, how kind of you to say so.

B: These are really great pictures you took Mr. James. Those of the sunset are magnificent.

A: Thank you, but with this camera taking good pictures is really easy. No skill on my part, I assure you.

Useful Expressions

Where would you go if you wanted to go on an island tour?
- go to a world renowned festival
- see a movie
- go scuba diving or snorkeling
- see the beauty of nature
- see animals
- go to eat
- go sailing
- see historical sites

- see Buddhist temples
- go surfing
- go shopping
- see works of art
- go to an amusement park
- see famous people

43
UNIT

Hotel Compliments 2

43

UNIT

Hotel Compliments 2

<Health and Leisure Staff>

A: You did a wonderful job of matching me with a golf partner. I appreciate it.
B: No problem at all, sir.
B: Excellent game Mr. James. You really gave me a workout.
A: Thanks, I guess all those private lessons are finally paying off.

<Housekeeping Staff>

A: The room is spotless. You do excellent work.
B: Thank you ma'am.
B: You are so tidy sir. You make it very easy to clean your room.
A: Well, as my mother always said, ''Cleanliness is next to Godliness''.

<Kitchen Staff>

A: My compliments to the chef. This linguine is superb.
B: Thank you ma'am. I'll appreciate any and all comments.
B: That recipe you shared with us was superb. I may even include it on the menu.
A: My pleasure and that would certainly be an honor.

<Spa Staff>

A: You have great hands my dear. I've never felt better.
B: Thank you sir, I appreciate that.
B: Your new hair-do looks absolutely gorgeous, Mrs. Susan.
A: Why··· thank you for noticing. My husband didn't.

44
UNIT

Hotel Staffs Etc.

44

UNIT

Hotel Staffs Etc.

What does America have for breakfast?

Imagine an American breakfast and what comes to mind? Ham and eggs, with hash browns? Pancakes with maple syrup and bacon? The reality tends to be simpler. Cereal and fruit juice have been breakfast staples for generations - though that now seems to be changing.

The breakfast cereal behemoth, Kellogg, announced in July that quarterly global earnings had fallen by a sizable 16% over the year before. That same month, orange juice sales plummeted to the lowest in a decade, according to the Florida Department of Citrus.

Two pillars of the everyday American breakfast, seen for decades as part of a well-rounded morning meal, seem to be slowly losing their appeal to US consumers. But what foods are Americans turning to instead?

One telling sign was the departure last year of the head of Kellogg's US breakfast-foods division, who took up the helm of yogurt maker Chobani Inc. As Kellogg's sales have dropped, Chobani's have skyrocketed to nearly $1bn a year.

Some 80% of Americans still eat breakfast inside the home, according to Balzer. An estimated 10% report they skip the meal entirely - people aged between 18 and 35 are most likely to do this - while another 10% get breakfast elsewhere.

And it's that last 10% that have restaurants in a feeding frenzy. In fact, the only area where the crowded restaurant industry has seen growth in the last decade has been on take-out breakfast, Balzer says.

McDonald's, which began selling the Egg McMuffin in 1971, is still king with more than 19% of all fast-food breakfast sales in the US - sales that are worth $40bn per year. Burger King gobbles up nearly 3%, according to the Wall Street Journal, but companies like Subway and Taco Bell are entering the fray with items such as the new "waffle taco".

Some consumers are looking for a low-fat, low-calorie breakfast, though, or one that matches their personal definition of what a "healthy" breakfast should be. One of the reasons cereal and orange juice have had the pulp beaten out of them is because of a shift away from sugar and carbohydrates toward yogurt and sandwiches with protein-rich fillings.

Breakfasters in Britain have also jumped on the higher-protein trend with eggs showing a 13.7% rise in consumption in the last year. Eggs' perfect partners, bacon and sausage, have also seen a rise in popularity as cereal sales declined, according to The Grocer.

In both countries, the link between weight loss and breakfast is constantly debated. Every year, conflicting studies are released touting breakfast as a must for fighting obesity, or skipping breakfast as the key to keep weight down.

Andrew Brown, a scientist at the The University of Alabama at Birmingham Nutrition and Obesity Research Center, investigated more than 100 different studies in this area and found there was no clear link.

Breakfast in the UK

- Cereal, tea and bread are the three most common breakfast items, though cereal and bread have been in long-term decline

- Eggs are now being eaten 13.7% more often at breakfast than they were a year ago - they feature in about one in 13 breakfasts - partly because of reports that they help people feel full for longer
- There has also been a 7.1% increase in bacon consumption at breakfast in the last six months
- One in three people regularly skip breakfast
- Consumption of on-the-go breakfast products - taken from home to be eaten elsewhere - was down 9% over the six months from December to May, compared with a year earlier

"There's a halo around breakfast, that if you want to lose weight, you have to eat breakfast," Brown says. "[But] there wasn't a lot of good strong evidence to support it."

What he and his colleagues did find was that American attitudes about breakfast have changed significantly over the last century.

In historical literature from the early 1900s, "you've got these gigantic breakfasts with steak and eggs and oatmeal - so many calories - and it talks about that you must have this energy or you'll waste away, that you need to be able to be fuelled for your day," he says.

"And now we look at the narrative and we're telling people you have to eat in the morning so you don't weigh as much," he says. The theory just wasn't borne out in his study's data.

One thing experts do appear to agree on is the difficulty in determining just what, exactly, Americans do eat for breakfast on any given day. The reason? Most people, when surveyed, tend to lie about it to avoid negative judgement.

According to Balzer, what people say they eat says just as much about them as, say, their choice in fashion. They say "what they want you to hear," he says. "They want you to hear they're eating quinoa."

What is a Continental Breakfast?[47]

A continental breakfast is a light morning meal that is provided by many hotels and motels. It traditionally includes bread products, fruit juice and hot beverages. Some lodging facilities also include other types of food, such as cereal, fruit, meat and eggs. The meal typically is presented in a buffet, from which guests can help themselves, rather than being served to the guests like it would be in a restaurant. The quality and amount of food that is provided can vary widely and often depends on the quality of the establishment, with high-end hotels that attract business travelers typically providing better continental breakfast food than roadside motels that attract families who are vacationing on tight budgets.

Origin of the Term

The term "continental breakfast" refers to the continent of Europe and distinguishes this simple breakfast from an English breakfast, which typically consists of more food and often includes meats, cereals, fruits and even vegetables in addition to bread products, juice and hot beverages. Light breakfasts such as those often enjoyed by people in Europe, especially France, are considered easier, cheaper and quicker for hotels to provide to their guests. It also is convenient for travelers who might not have time for a sit-down meal in the morning before needing to continue on their journey.

Serving Procedure

A continental breakfast usually is provided in the hotel or motel lobby, or in a room near the lobby, for a specified period of time during the morning. The food typically is placed on a large table or counter, and amenities such as plates, bowls, forks, spoons and knives are made available. There might be tables and chairs where guests can sit and eat, or they could take their breakfast back to their rooms or elsewhere.

47) Chuck, Ben. American Culture Heritage, pp.145

Breads

The bread products that are included in a continental breakfast might include toast, doughnuts, pastries, croissants and rolls. Pancakes or waffles are less likely to be included, although toaster waffles might be offered. Butter, assorted jams and jellies or other toppings, such as syrup for waffles, usually are available.

Beverages

Juices and hot beverages are almost always included in a continental breakfast. Orange juice, apple juice and grapefruit juice are common. Various types of coffee and tea usually are provided. Hot chocolate might be available for children or for guests who do not drink coffee or tea. Milk also is available sometimes.

Fruits and Cereals

The other foods that are included in a continental breakfast can vary widely. Some hotels provide fruit such as bananas, apples, oranges and grapefruits. Cold breakfast cereal and milk are often provided. Hot cereal, such as instant oatmeal, is sometimes available as well.

Rare Fare

It is more rare for cooked meats or eggs to be included in a continental breakfast, but it does happen. For example, large containers full of scrambled eggs, bacon or sausage links might be placed out for guests. Hash browns — fried shredded potatoes — are another cooked breakfast item that is sometimes available.

Tips for Guests

Most hotels that offer continental breakfasts will tell guests the time period when the food will be available. Many times, a limited amount of food will be provided each day. For this reason, guests who wait until near the end of the availability time period should expect that the supply of some items might be gone. Also, it is considered to be poor etiquette for a guest to take very large portions of the food that is provided. This type of breakfast is meant to be quick and light, not a full meal that will satiate a person's hunger for many hours.

Yes, they really shouldn't use the name "Continental" when the Motel/Hotel offers as much food as a full blown breakfast. Meaning coffee, juice, hot and cold cereals, fruit, pastries, bagels or muffins, eggs, bacon, sausage, waffles. You don't need any more than this for a complete breakfast. If you do, you have an eating disorder.

Continental in the past meant coffee or juice and either toast , pastry, muffin or bagel -- one or the other. Somehow, they added more food items but kept the name Continental. So I always call the place directly and ask what's included in their breakfast, no matter what name they use.

To the people complaining about others eating too much food: If you're going to be sitting on a bus all day and not eating until 3 in the afternoon, you're going to grab a larger portion of biscuits and gravy and a second piece of toast.

I stayed at a hotel once that offered as its continental breakfast one cinnamon roll (you weren't allowed more than one per person) and coffee.

As for being "greedy", when you're on the run and want to do a lot of things that day, you may end up skipping or delaying a later meal time so wanting a big breakfast is not out of the question.

Rclatcd Topics Contincntal Brcakfast Motcl Brcakfast Chcap Motcls Brcakfast Inn Conference Hotel

The funny thing is, that on the continent (assuming that means the western European countries) many hotels offer a breakfast which is included in the room fee and consists of coffee/tea, juice, different kinds of bread (varies with the country), cheese, sausage, spreads, egg (boiled as well as scrambled), ham, tomatoes, cucumbers, peppers, cereals, sweets, etc.

By the way, donuts aren't continental at all. Being continental myself, I experience the "continental breakfast" as being very strange.

I suppose it depends on the continent you are on, but continental breakfast originally meant coffee and pastries or breads. Because of competition for hotel rooms, properties are consistently trying to outdo each other. But it's breakfast, not continental breakfast anymore.

It varies by the hotel chain. Parts of the Choice network offer the hot breakfasts and call it continental, while other part of the chain are not required to offer anything for breakfast at all.

I manage a smaller branded hotel. We customize the breakfast to the price being paid. During the slower months when the business is down, I offer toast, muffins, danishes, honey buns, cereal, etc. But for major events when we rent for 200 per night, they have more options, like bagels, eggs, etc.

Related Topics Continental Breakfast Motel Breakfast Cheap Motels Breakfast Inn Conference Hotel

Raises eyebrow.* It's sad when a breakfast menu turns political. No matter what administration or political affiliation, I can't imagine the breakfast that is being served at a hotel has anything to do with the White House.

If you're going to criticize the current administration then criticize them for things they've actually done. Hotel breakfast offerings as well as everything else a hotel does or does not do boils down to profit - period.

Blame it on the United States federal government and Michelle Obama's obsession with telling us what we can and can't eat. Hotels couldn't serve bacon and eggs if they wanted to, because Michelle Obama wants to control what we eat. Oh well, 2012 is right around the corner!

A continental breakfast for no charge is a minor convenience offered by most economy priced hotels today. It was never intended to be confused with a full hot breakfast that people actually pay for at a restaurant. If a hotel advertises a continental breakfast, people should not be disappointed if they aren't served bacon and eggs. Most hotels can't afford to offer a free full breakfast because people are just too greedy. Ever see anyone at a salad bar or buffet without food piled high on their plate?

A hotel is not a free, all you can eat restaurant, but some people think it should be after they shop around to save $10 off the room. If you expect to have an all you can eat buffet for breakfast, then don't expect to get the lowest priced room in town. Nothing is really free.

It's something called cultural differences. Most Americans do not eat boiled eggs for breakfast. They eat them scrambled, fried, poached or in something else, but rarely boiled. I never eat boiled eggs if I can help it. I don't like them. Many Americans (including me) also appreciate fresh fruit and/or muffins for breakfast.

When I was in Aruba, our hotel offered a variety of items for breakfast, in keeping with the visitors they have from all over the world. There was a hot buffet, cold meats and cheeses, muesli, various breads, and an omelette station, as well as fruit.

I am a Southerner, but I don't expect to find biscuits (the hot bread) everywhere when I am not in

What does a muffin have to do with a continental breakfast? What does a continental breakfast served in USA have to do with a real continental breakfast? - nothing!

I do not understand why a continental breakfast is considered to include only coffee/tea, fruit and croissant in USA (and even muffins). In Europe we are used to eating (and it is always available in hotels) for breakfast: bread/toast/croissant, ham, salami, cheese, marmalade, boiled egg, bagels, pastries, cakes, cookies, yogurt, milk, coffee, juice, tea, oatmeal, cereal ... and you got as much as you wish.

Here, in the Washington in hotel Madera, for the continental breakfast i got to choose between tea and coffee, croissant and muffin, and I got fruit. Crazy combination. The other kinds of breakfast (I suppose American?) contained always egg in any kind but boiled.

The two hotels I stayed in Italy this summer had both excellent breakfast offers. The Hilton hotel in Rome had such a wide variety of foods that could please almost any guest. They even included oatmeal, by request, my favorite breakfast food.

Another hotel in southern Italy, near Sorento had similarly generous breakfast foods. It is really nice to get up in the morning and have a good breakfast waiting for you.

The last time I stayed at a hotel which was about two months ago in new jersey they served omelets, bagels, cereal, bacon, ham, coffee, juice, granola bars and fruits and yogurt. i was quite surprised. i would have thought it would have been cereal and milk and juice but it was much better.

I'm going to Kissimmee, florida this upcoming friday and I'm praying and hoping to God that the hotel i will be staying at for two weeks will come with the same friendly and hospitable service that the Howard johnson hotel had. Hope this comment helped or at least give you an idea of which hotel is clean affordable and has a scrumptious choice of cuisine God bless you all! Janny

There is also the option to use a toaster, microwave, and not forgetting fruits: apples, bananas, oranges (in Florida), etc.

I've found that, too - the "continental breakfast" is getting fancier. The last hotel I stayed at that had a free continental breakfast had an omelet chef for a couple hours. Otherwise it was just cereal and muffins, and scrambled eggs in a pan, buffet style. I'll definitely remember that when I need to stay in a hotel again, though! [48)]

Some hotels offer a bit more substantial continental breakfast, where they might include such things as smoked salmon, hard boiled eggs, a variety of cheeses and cold cuts. Seasonal fresh fruit might also be included, and all of that can make for a well rounded breakfast.

---

48) • It tastes stale!
- I couldn't help it. They were so good!
- How do you want your beef?
- Make it small, please.
- I want it to be very, very lean.
- How often do you eat out?
- I'd like to reserve a table for dinner.
- It's on me.
- It's my treat.
- A drink to you and your future wife!

45
UNIT

Hotel Introduction

45

UNIT

Hotel Introduction

Dialogue 1

A: Mr. James, I'd like you to meet Dr. John.

B: It's nice to meet you, Dr. John.

C: Pleasure to meet you, too.

A: Dr. John is an economist. He just finished writing a book on international trade.

D: Oh? That's my field, too. I work for the Korean assembly.

C: In the Development Program, by any chance?

D: Yes. How did you guess?

C: I've read your articles on technical assistance. They're excellent.

Dialogue 2

A: Thanks for dinner! It was delicious!

B: It's OK.

A: Next time lunch is on me.

B: Don't be silly.

A: I'm serious.

B: All right. Next time you'll treat.

Dialogue 3

A: James, where are the cookies? Don't tell me you ate them all! Again!

B: Yes, I did. I couldn't help it. They were so good.

A: I thought you didn't like cookies.

B: Well, I don't like cookies flavored with chocolate at all. But vanilla is different. I love them to death.

A: Huh, I didn't know that.

B: Well, tell you what, vanilla cookies taste even better with a glass of cold milk.

Dialogue 4

A: James, can you do me a favor? Can you help me cut this chicken?

B: At your service. How do you want me to cut it?

A: I would like half of it cut into slices, and the other half diced.

B: OK. Half sliced and the other half diced.

A: Oh, by the way, I want it to be very, very lean. Not even a shred of fat.

B: Got'cha. Cut off the fat.

46
UNIT

Ordering a meal

46

UNIT

Ordering a meal

Dialogue 1

A: Hi, I'll be your waiter today. Can I start you off with something to drink?

B: Yes. I'll have iced coke, please.

C: And I'll have orange juice.

A: OK. Are you ready to order, or do you need a few minutes?

B: I think we're ready. I'll have the tomato soup to start, and the roast beef with mashed potatoes and peas.

A: How do you want the beef — rare, medium, or well done?

B: Medium, please.

---

49) • Can you keep an eye on my bag?
- You should've kept an eye on it.
- Can you save my place, please?
- Is this seat taken?
- I really miss the comforts of home!
- East or west, home is the best.
- I'm low on gas.
- We're only staying overnight.

C: And I'll just have the fish, with potatoes and a salad.
A: Thank you

Dialogue 2

A: I heard you took a trip to LA.
B: Yes, I did.
A: How did you like it?
B: Oh, I got sick and tired of hotels and hotel food.
A: I can imagine. East or west, home is the best.

Dialogue 3

A: Excuse me, can you do me a favor?
B: Sure. What can I do for you?
A: Can you save my place for me, please?
B: Sure. But hurry. The line is moving fast.
A: Thanks. It won't be long. I'll be right back.

Dialogue 4

A: Where is my backpack?
B: I don't know. Where did you leave it?
A: I just put it on the chair a while ago, but now it's gone.
B: Are you sure?
A: Of course, I'm sure! I bet someone stole it.
B: Well, you should've kept an eye on it.

47
UNIT

At the doctor's office

47

UNIT

At the doctor's office

Dialogue 1

A: What seems to be the problem?

B: Well, I have a bad cough and a sore throat. I also have a headache.

A: How long have you had these symptoms?

B: About five days now. And I'm really tired, too.

A: It sounds like you've got the flu. Take aspirin every five hours and get plenty of rest. Make sure you drink lots of fluids. Call me if you're still sick next week.

B: OK, thank you.

---

50) • Someone has a crush on Esther.
• I think he's my Mr. Right!
• I heard you're going out with Susan.
• He's head over heels in love with you.
• There's plenty of fish in the sea.
• I'm breaking up with her.
• I just can't get it off my mind.
• We're not seeing each other any more.

Dialogue 2

A: Hi, James, we're having a party tonight, wanna come join us? You can bring your girlfriend.

B: Well...I'm breaking up with Esther.

A: What happened? Did you have a fight?

B: No. She's really a very nice girl....

A: Yeah, she is. She's pretty, caring, and easy-going. And she's a great cook! She's a gem!

B: Well, you're right. But sometimes she's too caring... well... no... she's just possessive... and... uh... I kind of want a break... you know... for some room for myself.

A: Oh?! Did you talk with her about it?

B: I've tried, but...it didn't work.

A: Oh. So, when are you going to tell her?

B: Maybe tonight. I don't know. I don't know how to tell her.

A: I know she's head over heels in love with you. She'll be badly hurt!

B: I know....

Dialogue 3

A: Hi, James. Haven't seen you for a while? How is Esther?

B: We're not seeing each other any more.

A: What happened? Did you break up?

B: Yeah. I got sick and tired of her nagging all the time.

A: Oh, I'm sorry. Maybe, you were just emotional at that moment. Do you think you guys can get back together?

B: I don't know. There's plenty of fish out there in the sea.

A: Oh, you're such a dog!

48
UNIT

Your Favorite Sport

48

UNIT

Your Favorite Sport

Dialogue 1

A: What time is that baseball game on? I thought it started at 2.

B: We must have had the wrong time. Oh, well ··· baseball's not my favorite sport anyway. I much prefer tennis.

A: Oh, really? I thought your favorite sport was baseball.
I'm a big fan of volleyball, too.

B: How about a game sometime?

A: Sure thing! Why don't we go shoot some hoops now since the baseball game isn't on?

B: Excellent idea. Let's go.

A: OK.

---

51) • We've got three holidays in a row!
- I guess I can put it off until next month.
- I'm through for the summer.
- I wish I could get away for a while.
- It's good relax.

Dialogue 2

A: I'm so glad the weekend's finally here.
B: Me too. Imagine. It's a long weekend. We've got two days in a row.
A: So, where're you going?
B: I don't have any plans yet. I'll just play it by ear. How about you?
A: We're going to go hiking and camping in the mountains.
B: That sounds exciting!
A: Wanna join us?
B: Let me think about it. I'll let you know later.

Dialogue 3

A: Do you have school today?
B: I'm through for the summer.
A: Really? So what do you plan to do?
B: Well, I don't know what I'm going to do with my free time yet.
A: Are you planning to take any summer classes?
B: No. I think I'll just relax. I really need a break. A long break!

49
UNIT

Post office

49

UNIT

Post office

Dialogue 1

A: Hello. What can I do for you?

B: OK. I need to mail this package to Seoul, please.

A: OK, let's see how much it weighs ··· it's about 10 pounds. If you send it express, it will get there next monday. Or you can send it priority and it will get there by friday.

B: Next monday is fine. How much will that be?

A: 20 dollars. Do you need anything else?

B: Oh, yeah! I almost forgot. I need a book of stamps, too.

A: OK, your total comes to 35 dollars.

52) • A drink to our friendship!
- Don't forget to drop me a line!
- It's hard to keep up contact!
- Why don't you have a heart-to-heart talk with her?
- Honesty is the best policy.

Dialogue 2

A: How are things going with you and your roommate?

B: Not very well. We're supposed to share the groceries, but I end up feeding him three meals a day. My grocery bill is huge, you know. I really can't afford it any longer.

A: I know how you feel. I used to have a roommate like that. He never offered to reimburse me for anything.

B: I'm really fed up with his freeloading, but I just don't know how to tell him that he should come up with half the grocery bill, because sometimes he treats me to a meal in a restaurant.

A: Well, honesty is the best policy. Maybe you just want to have a heart-to-heart, friend-to-friend talk with him. If he refuses to mend his ways, then ask him to move out. You can't let him wear out his welcome.

Dialogue 3

A: I heard you're moving to LA.

B: Yes. I've got an offer in LA.

A: Oh, that's great! But I'm going to miss you.

B: Me, too. Let's keep in touch.

A: Yeah. Don't forget to drop me a line when you settle down.

B: Trust me. I won't. I'll keep you posted.

A: You have my address?

B: Well, I have your e-mail address.

A: All right! I look forward to hearing from you soon. Good luck!

UNIT 50

At the supermarket

50

UNIT

At the supermarket

Dialogue 1

A: Hey, James ··· Look at those desserts! How about baking some cookies today?

B: Hmm ··· Yeah, that's a good idea! While we're here, let's pick up the ingredients. OK, what do we need?

A: The recipe calls for flour, sugar and butter. Oh, and we also need eggs and chocolate chips.

B: Why don't you get the dairy ingredients? You'll find those in the refrigerated section in the back of the store.

I'll get the dry ingredients — they're in aisle 15.

A: Good. Let's meet at the checkout.

B: OK. See you there

53) • Why does she have a long face?
- Chances are slim!
- I am overwhelmed with a heavy workload.
- Once you get the hang of it....
- I'll keep that in mind.
- I believe I have a good chance.

Dialogue 2

A: What are the chances of getting a raise this year?

B: Chances are slim!

A: Wow! You haven't gotten a raise for how many years now?

B: It's been three years! The company keeps losing money and they can't afford to give anyone a raise.

A: That's too bad. Did you ever think of working somewhere else?

B: Yeah. In fact, I have an interview next Friday.

A: Good luck!

Dialogue 3

A: Hi, James. I heard you're looking for a new job.

B: Yeah. I just had an interview yesterday.

A: Oh. How did it go?

B: I think I did well. They said they would make a decision by this Saturday.

A: This Saturday? Looks like they want to hire the person as quickly as possible.

B: Yeah! I think so, too.

A: What are your chances of getting that job?

B: I believe I have a very good chance. The director seems to like me.

A: Well, good luck, then.

B: Thanks. I hope it helps.

51
UNIT

Calling for help

51

UNIT

Calling for help

Dialogue 1

A: Hey! That car just ran a red light and hit that truck!

B: Is anyone hurt?

A: I don't know ··· let's call 119. ··· Hello? I'd like to report a car accident near the post office on James Street.
It looks like a woman is hurt. Yes, it just happened. OK, Thank you. Bye.

B: What did they say?

A: They're going to send an ambulance and a police car right away.

B: Good, they're here. I hope the woman is OK.

A: I know. You have to be so careful when you're driving.

B: Thank you.

---

54) • Her skin looks so newborn baby smooth!
• The razor burn is really irritating.
• It knocks out bacteria and fungi.
• Why! Age has set in!
• I'm ready for a lift.

Dialogue 2

A: My toes feel very itchy. It's really irritating. I don't know what's happening.

B: Let me take a look. Ah-huh, I think you have athlete's foot.

A: What are you talking about? I'm not an athlete!

B: Come on, John, stop joking. You'd better take care of it before it gets worse. Imagine you have pus gushing out and rashes all over your legs....

A: Stop it, "Dr." James.

B: OK, OK. I guess I've got some cream for it. It really fixes skin in trouble. It's really a help for irritations and blemishes.

A: Is it this one?

B: Not really. That one is for heat burns.

A: Have you had athlete's foot before?

B: Yeah. It was a very bad experience. You know, if you don't keep your feet dry and clean, the fungus will grow and spread out quickly.

A: So my case isn't that bad, huh?

B: You're lucky. Yeah, here it is. Now apply it to the affected areas. This cream is very effective in clearing out bacteria and stopping inflammation from developing.

Dialogue 3

A: Hello. How are you doing?
Do you know anyone who's had plastic surgery?

B: I'm okay. Thank you.
You mean like a breast enlargement? I don't think that's really necessary. That's not the way a woman should stay attractive.

A: Why not? Why can't we go back to the way things were?

B: Because! I don't know! But, James, you wouldn't do that, would you?

A: Darned right I would!

B: Maybe make-up would be enough?

A: Come on, Susan. Be open-minded! Look at my eyes! They're puffy. And my eyebags, they're dark and loose and full of lines and circles. I really hope surgery can wipe out the tired feelings.

B: But what would other people think?

A: I don't care what other people think. I'm ready for a lift.

B: OK.

A: Thanks.

B: Have a good day.

A: Thank you. You too, sir.

Bibliography

강덕윤 · 고동완 · 이정욱.(2014). 호텔 카지노 기본회화. 백산출판사
방기준(1997). 관광생활영어 정문각
함영덕.(2012). 관광생활영어. 백산출판사
홍일출(2015). 항공영어. 백산출판사
Alpa, Guido. Tradition and Europeanization in Italian Law. London: British Institute of International and Comparative Law, 2005.
Amin, Ash and John Tomany. Behind the Myth of European Union: Prospects for Cohesion. New York: 1995.
Andersen, Svein S. and Kjell A. Eliassen. The European Union, How Democratic Is It? Thousand Oaks, CA: Sage, 1996.
Antoniolli, Luisa. "Principles of European Contract Law and Italian Law." In Principles of European Contract Law. Edited by Anna Veneziano. The Hague: Kluwer Law International, 2005.
Bonasio, A. (2015). Textual Analysis - Hotel Rwanda. [online] Academia.edu. Available at: http://www.academia.edu/273378/Textual_Analysis_-_Hotel_Rwanda [Accessed 20 Jan. 2015].
Bickmore, T. and Cassell, J. (2005). Social Dialogue with Embodied Conversational Agents. New York: Kluwer Academic, p.3.
Noh Sun Hee (2016). Real English for Hotel Staff, DARAKWON
Liddicoat, A. (2011). An introduction to conversation analysis. London: Continuum.
Pease, A. (2004). The definitive book of body language. Australia: Pease International.
James. K Park. (2016). Tourism English Conversation, Back San
Wolfram, W. and Schilling-Estes, N. (1998). American English. Malden, Mass.: Blackwell Publishers.
Wong, J. and Waring, H. (2010). Conversation analysis and second language pedagogy. New York: Routledge.
www.kyoboacademy.co.kr/academy/product/bookInfo.laf?barcode=978..

저자약력

김종견(문학박사)

미국 캘리포니아 주립 SBVC 대학
연세대학교 경영학과 졸업
미국 캘리포니아 Azusa. P Univ. 대학원 졸업
고려대학교 대학원 영문과
미국 캘리포니아 BCC 대학원 졸업

미국 Bethel Christian Center Ordained Minister
해양수산부 정책자문위원 역임
농림축산식품부 일반농산어촌개발사업 평가위원
강원도 기업형새농촌 평가위원
사단법인 강원발전정책포럼 회장
사단법인 녹색전국연합 원주지회장 등

저자와의
합의하에
인지첩부
생략

Practical Hotel English

2021년 8월 20일 초판 1쇄 인쇄
2021년 8월 25일 초판 1쇄 발행

저　자 김종견
펴낸이 진욱상
펴낸곳 백산출판사
교　정 박시내
본문디자인 오행복
표지디자인 오정은

등　록 1974년 1월 9일 제406-1974-000001호
주　소 경기도 파주시 회동길 370(백산빌딩 3층)
전　화 02-914-1621(代)
팩　스 031-955-9911
이메일 edit@ibaeksan.kr
홈페이지 www.ibaeksan.kr

ISBN 979-11-6639-187-3　13740
값 20,000원